C000180904

The Golf Widow's Guide
to Short Breaks
in the UK

The Golf Widow's Guide
to Short Breaks
in the UK

SALLY McILROY

THE CHOIR PRESS

Copyright © 2022 Sally McIlroy

All rights reserved. No part of this publication may be reproduced or transmitted in any form or by any means, electronic or mechanical including photocopying, recording or any information storage or retrieval system, without prior permission in writing from the publishers.

The right of Sally McIlroy to be identified as the author of this work has been asserted by her in accordance with the Copyright, Designs and Patents Act 1988

First published in the United Kingdom in 2022 by
The Choir Press

ISBN 978-1-78963-330-6

18 ~~holes~~ *short breaks*

Introduction

Golf is more than a game, it is a lifestyle. It ticks all the boxes in terms of health and wellbeing, and a passionate golfer is never without a purpose. The problem is a round of golf, including the post-game drink, can take several hours. Add to this trips to play on courses some distance from home, regular viewing of all the big tournaments, and various golf club events, and it leaves little spare time.

As a golf widow I am pleased for my husband, but in the meantime want to maximise the enjoyment in my own life before it is too late. This book is a personal account of short breaks that I have taken – that aren't linked to golf – that I think other sports widows will enjoy. The hope is that the book will make a refreshing change from conventional travel guides because, like a good restaurant where taster menus have taken over from a la carte, this provides a carefully sourced set choice and includes a recommended book linked to each destination.

Each trip averages two nights away, with transport predominately by car. Some of the accommodation is extremely basic (a Benedictine Abbey in Hereford), others more luxurious (the best hotel in Alnwick), but overall justifiable when compared with the cost of a round of golf!

Every journey is special in that you are directed to places not always mentioned elsewhere. Examples include a village evacuated in 1943, a stunning interiors store based around the Japanese concept of embracing imperfection, and an old fashioned pier where polished brass plaques pinned to the deck will make you laugh and cry in equal measure. Enjoy – if only for the lovely illustrations drawn mainly by local artists.

Sally McIlroy

A WALK AROUND
LUDLOW

LUDLOW FOOD CENTRE

LUDLOW TOWN F.C.

LUDLOW RACE COURSE

RIVER CORVE

LEISURE CENTRE

THE BOILING WELL

LUDLOW CRICKET CLUB

LUDLOW CEMETERY

LUDLOW COMMUNITY HOSPITAL

THE UNICORN INN

RUGBY FOOTBALL CLUB

LUDLOW BREWING CO.

ST LAURENCE'S CHURCH

LUDLOW LIBRARY

RAIL STATION

LUDLOW CASTLE

LINNEY RIVERSIDE PARK

LUDLOW COLLEGE

THE ROSE & CROWN

THE FEATHERS HOTEL

THE CHURCH INN

FOOD FESTIVAL

MARKET

LUDLOW MUSEUM & BUTTERCROSS

CASTLE LODGE

LUDLOW ASSEMBLY ROOMS

BODENHAMS

THE GREEN CAFE

DINHAM HALL HOTEL

YE OLD BULL RING TAVERN

THE QUEENS PUB

THE WHEATSHEAF INN

RIVER TEME

WHITCLIFFE COMMON NATURE RESERVE

THE BLUE BOAR

MASCALL CENTRE

THE CHARLTON ARMS

WEIR BRIDGE

MONKEY MANIA SOFT PLAY

The illustration is by Mercedes Leon

Ludlow in Shropshire

Recommended read: *Dead Ground in Between*
by Maureen Jennings, a rather old fashioned but enjoyable
story set in the Clee Hills near Ludlow

The Ludlow trip is a gem, but you need to get organised first. Accommodation is in a Georgian rectory with wonderful views, divine beds and the gentlest black Labrador imaginable. You will then dip into medieval England, and finally receive a guided tour of a mansion that was the setting of the film *Atonement*. This last is the organised bit as tours of Stokesay Court take place less than once a week, and booking is by the process of sending a cheque to the lovely Caroline.

Accommodation:

The Old Rectory in Wheathill is a short drive from Ludlow and in the middle of nowhere. From the minute you put your bag down in either the Blue, Green or Yellow room you will relax. Once unpacked, afternoon tea is served (in the garden – weather is permitting) and you will then get a chance to meet Charcoal. The accommodation is bed and breakfast, but soup and a sandwich (or indeed a candle-lit dinner) is on offer later should you wish, and nothing is particularly expensive. I've stayed in places triple the price – not on my own I hasten to add – that are less than half as nice. The address is Wheathill, Ludlow, WV16 6QT, the phone number 01746 787209 (theoldrectorywheathill.com).

This trip was particularly special to me because over breakfast (on the lovely terrace), I met a delightful elderly lady who had booked to come with her daughter but due to work commitments had to pull out at the last minute. She said that she very nearly didn't come as it felt strange going to places and eating out alone. I discovered what an amazing life and career she had had in her youth, yet retirement had sapped all her confidence. How easy it is to succumb to self-doubt – unless you fight it.

Ludlow:

Described by Sir John Betjeman as 'Probably the loveliest town in England', my first impression was of how exceptionally 'nice' everyone was. Arriving at lunchtime I had a salad down an alleyway off Curve Street and was served by a friendly waitress. It was a very hot day and they had sold out of cold drinks, but instead of grumbling, there were offers of help from the customers to nip down to the supermarket to buy some more. On the walk back to my car I saw a Swap Box which was for Ludlow residents to put in surplus produce from their garden or homemade jam etc. to share with others. Similarly, outside the local delicatessens a Help Yourself tray was sitting by the door full of pretty olive tins and coffee grounds ... to keep slugs at bay. There really is something exceptional about Ludlow.

A brief history:

The settlement of Ludlow began with the building of the castle around 1086 by Roger De Lacy as a Welsh border stronghold. In the twelfth century the town was laid out to provide services to the garrison and as a source of income to the manorial lord. In 1230 a wall was built around this new Norman town with seven gates, although only one remains today in Broad Street. As time passed, the castle was added to and in the 14th century it became a magnificent palace. Later, under the ownership of the duke of York, the castle was involved in the War of the Roses. In 1501, Prince Arthur (brother of Henry VIII) honeymooned here with his bride, Catherine of Aragon, before his early death. By the late 1600s, the Royal Welsh Fusiliers had arrived and it was abandoned soon after and fell into decay. Today it is privately owned but open to visitors.

Ludlow has always been a wealthy town, and this was due to the lucrative wool and cloth trade (pre-1600), followed by tanning and glove making. It became a fashionable resort to visit and the Ludlow 'season' played a part in establishing many fine Georgian town houses. Some of the houses have a Georgian front superimposed on a medieval behind, and it is this mix of medieval and Georgian housing stock that makes the place feel so special. There are 500 listed buildings in Ludlow and a good book to dip into whilst you are there is *The Time Traveller's Guide to Medieval England* by Ian Mortimer.

Not to miss when you visit Ludlow, and ideally in the following order (but don't dwell too long as this trip is full on):

Ludlow Castle

The castle is to be found at the top of the town near the market and there is parking nearby. It opens at 10am daily except in January to mid-February when it is just open at weekends (ludlowcastle.com). There are views over the countryside from the tower but the key thing to see is the Round Chapel. It is one of the few circular surviving naves in Britain and was dedicated to St Mary Magdelene. An information board explains the history, as does another nearby about the North Range and Great Hall in Mortimer's Palace. It was from this castle in 1483 that young Prince Edward made his ill-fated journey to the capital that would end – not in accession to the throne, but in his murder in the Tower of London.

Dinham House

This is signposted from the castle on the route to Dinham Mill. It is an 18th century town house used by the 'Knights of Downton, the Johnes of Croft Castle, and Earles of Powis'. Lucien Bonaparte was a prisoner here in 1811. There is no charge to wander round, as it is a showroom for Clearview Stoves. It illustrates the essence of living in a well-proportioned English country house and there is a room dedicated to explaining its history. From here stroll down towards the river, stopping briefly to look in at the Chapel of St Thomas c.1190.

Dinham Mill and Ludlow Millennium Green

There has been a mill here on the Teme for nearly 700 years. It was at the cutting edge of medieval technology. Two wheels turned grindstones to grind corn into flour, and later the water power was harnessed to meet the needs of the Industrial Revolution with an iron and brass foundry. This was followed by the new Electric Light Company in the early twentieth century. In more recent times the mill building became the changing rooms for swimming nearby. Now it houses the Green Café, a workshop and a meeting room. The green and the river front are a site of special scientific interest and form part of the conservation area. It is a lovely spot for a picnic and the café sells a delicious damson and sloe gin ice cream.

A stroll around the town

You can pick up a leaflet in the tourist information centre with suggested Ludlow walks, but the Ludlow Civic Society have positioned blue plaques on all the key buildings so that a leisurely stroll around this compact town (together with Merecedes' illustrated map) means that it really isn't necessary. There are numerous antique shops and art-related establishments. One such had a Lowry in its window when I was there, which indicates the quality, but in a shop opposite were pretty handmade chess sets, so there is something for everyone (almost). Look out for the Feathers on Corve Street, an early 17th century building, the home of Rees Jones, a self-made attorney at the Council of the Marches, who was keen to advertise his worldly success. It became an inn in 1670.

St Laurence's Parish Church

Positioned in the centre of the town off King Street, this is one of the largest parish churches in England. The foundations are twelfth century, but it was mostly rebuilt between 1344 and 1471. The interiors feature wood panelling and lovely stained-glass windows, not to mention wonderful radiators. Two places to see here are the Parvis room, which is above the porch and is being painstakingly renovated to reveal ancient coloured drawings, and the tower. The latter has 200 steps to the top but the views of the town and surrounding countryside from the top are worth it. Explore the churchyard next, (apparently the poet AE Housman is buried here, but I couldn't find his grave – you might have better luck). Similarly, look out for the half-timbered Reader's House and an interesting note about the Jubilee Garden next door.

Recommended places to eat in Ludlow include the Charlton Arms, which is on the river 01584 872813 (thecharltonarms.co.uk), Elliots

Bistro by the castle 01584 876464 (info@dinhamhall.com) and the French Pantry 01584 879133 at 15 Tower Street. The latter was fully booked for both nights when I visited and the reviews are amazing, but I notice it is quietly for sale so you might be out of luck.

Other destinations on your visit:

The Clee Hills

On one of the journeys back to your accommodation, instead of turning off onto the B road that takes you to the Old Rectory, continue straight on to reach the signposted Clee Hills. The scenery changes quite rapidly and before long you are crossing a sheep grid and are in the clouds. The social history of this area is fascinating and it is all explained in a book by Alfred Jenkins MBE who is now in his eighties. His publican father was a wheelwright, a carpenter and an undertaker. Basically the hills were mined for coal and subsequently granite for road sets. It was a hard life, and this much will be evident when you see it.

Thinking of historic characters, I had planned to include a fabulous illustrated map by the Shropshire artist and illustrator Katy Alston. It

is a rather special watercolour which shows historic characters linked to the area. Unfortunately it was too large to include, but on page 5 is a taste (note the humour – Captain Webb, 'sorry 'bout the puddle', swam the channel unaided in 1875).

Stokesay Court

Hopefully you have followed the instructions and booked tickets for a 2.30pm Tuesday tour via the owner, Caroline. The website is stokesaycourt.com and the address Onibury, Nr Craven Arms, SY7 9BD. The tour starts with a short film and ends with a cream tea in an oak panelled room overlooking the garden. Everything is explained on the tour but in summary: it was built for John Derby Allcroft, a wealthy glove manufacturer, and completed in 1892. It was one of the first private homes in England to be equipped with integral electric light. During the First World War it was used as an auxiliary military hospital, then in World War II it became a Western Command junior leaders' school. The present owner inherited the estate in a rather rundown state, but on being approached to host the film *Atonement*, her fortunes changed in that large areas of the house were renovated as part of the process.

Stokesay Castle

It is important to arrive at Stokesay Court on time as it starts promptly, and once the door is closed you are denied entry. So my suggestion, therefore, is that you might like to leave more than enough time to get there, which will enable you to very briefly nip into the fortified manor house that is rather inappropriately called a castle, and/or visit the church next door. The castle is an English Heritage property and was built in the 13th century by Laurence of Ludlow, an extremely wealthy wool merchant. It is just a short drive from Stokesay Court and is open daily from 10am until 6pm from April 1st to September 30th (check the opening times for other months of the year). The address is Stokesay, Craven Arms, SY7 9AH. Then on your way back from visiting both the castle and Stokesay Court, do stop at the Ludlow Food Centre, which you will pass on the A49, and buy one of their best sellers – a gold award-winning hand-cut marmalade.

On your journey home if you have time:

Carding Mill Valley

Church Stretton and Carding Mill Valley don't get much attention in the guide books, but I was pleased to swing by. Church Stretton is a small town that dates back to Anglo-Saxon times and is mentioned in the Doomsday Book. After a fire in 1593 many of the properties were rebuilt, so its appearance is slightly deceptive. It was an important staging post for mail and stage coaches between Liverpool and Bristol, but now it sees minibuses squeezing down the narrow lanes to the valley beyond. Indeed, Carding Mill valley is a haven for walkers, geography trips and nature lovers. The National Trust manages the site and there are leaflets with varying length walks freely available in the shop near the carpark. There is also a café. The postcode is SY6 6JG email cardingmill@nationaltrust.org.uk.

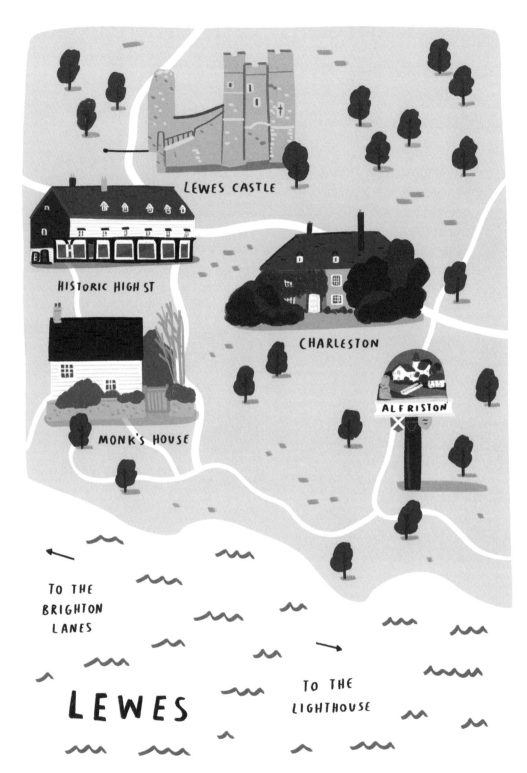

The illustration is by Alex Foster

Lewes in East Sussex

Recommended read: *To the Lighthouse* by Virginia Woolf

L ewes is the county town of East Sussex and is the perfect place to visit because it is compact, extremely historic and has a very independent identity. William Morris wrote in the mid-1800s:

> *'You can see Lewes lying like a box of toys under a great amphitheatre of chalk hills … on the whole it is set down better than any town I have seen in England.'*

Depending on where you are travelling from, this short trip can be one night or two (visit from April, and avoid Monday and Tuesday). It is important to book Charleston Farmhouse and Monk's House before you go otherwise you will miss the best two gems.

If you want to stay in town, the hotels are Pelham House in St Andrew's Lane, and the Shelleys at the top of the high street. I stayed in the former but didn't find it very relaxing. The latter dates back to 1588 and is a listed building with all the trappings of a grand house, however, for total peace and quiet (on this busy trip) it is best to stay just outside Lewes.

Accommodation:

My recommendation for this trip therefore, is to stay at Wingrove House in Alfriston. It is a 19th century colonial-style country house, which is well cared for by the owner and beautifully decorated. It is marketed as a 'restaurant with rooms' and is located in the high street, but tucked away so that you can sleep at night. The website is wingrovehousealfriston.com and the post code BN26 5TD. When I arrived to take a look, it was getting a thorough clean (always a good sign) and a couple climbing into their car said, 'We have been coming here for years. Can't fault it.'

The village is a beauty, in fact the hymn 'Morning Has Broken' was written there in 1931 by Eleanor Farjeon, based around the views. There is a quaint village store which has its wares laid out on wooden slats and where 'Bev, Rob and staff invite you to step inside for a little taste of history'. There is also a book shop, an art gallery, gift shops, tea rooms and the Gun Room (said to be the gun store for the Duke of Wellington).

More about Lewes:

Lewes began as a Saxon village built on a spur on the Downs, and its name probably derived from 'hluews', meaning slopes or hills. The Saxons built fortifications in the form of town walls and a mound, and it proved to be a sheltered and protected spot from civil unrest in the north. In Norman times, it couldn't avoid the Norman invasion and William the Conquer gave Lewes to one of his most powerful barons William de Warrenne. The fortifications were increased and Lewes Castle built. The Battle of Lewes took place in 1264 and was between Henry III and Simon de Montford; the town subsequently remained in the hands of the barons. The intervening period to the mid-1500s was difficult, with outbreaks of the plague, and the execution of Protestant martyrs who were burnt at the stake (outside the Star Inn, now the town hall), but the medieval street patterns became established, which lends much to the character of the town today.

In the 18th century Lewes was a busy little port and the principle town of Sussex with iron, brewing and ship building industries. Today it is famous for bonfire night. It is the biggest celebrated fifth of November event in the world (allegedly). Natasha Kaplinsky, who hails from Lewes, describes it as 'terrifying'. Thousands invade this otherwise sleepy town and horrible effigies are paraded around the town. So unless you have a penchant for fireworks, I would avoid visiting then.

Not to miss when you visit:

Lewes High Street

A pleasurable short day can be had in the town after a leisurely drive up from Alfriston. It is worth parking at the top of the town and working your way down. I have highlighted some places to see below but suggest you download 'A walk along the High Street' Lewes Heritage from the Friends of Lewes. It has a map, photographs of what to look out for, and goes into a lot of detail.

Start at Lewes Old Grammar School, which is at 140 High Street. It was founded in 1512 and notable former pupils include John Evelyn the diarist, and Wynne Edwin Baxter, coroner of the Whitechapel murders. There is a gallery opposite, and a few yards down a beautiful stone-inlaid lane leading to Anne of Cleves house. This is a 15th century timber-framed Wealden hall-house that was given to Anne as part of her divorce settlement from Henry VIII. It displays authentically furnished rooms, a traditional Tudor planted garden, and a local history museum. It is open daily from 1st February to 18th December at 10am (11am on Sundays), 52 Southover High Street, BN7 1JA (sussexpast.co.uk). Back to the high street and there are some lovely shops to visit as you stroll down towards the river. Notably, Paul Clark Clothiers at number 94, which has a ladies' store on one side of the road and men's on the other. It sells the sort of clothes that you might see in Liberty London but at a fraction of the cost. Also noteworthy is Flint at number 49, a lifestyle store housed inside a lovely 14th century timber building, and Closet & Botts, an old-style interiors store at number 196 High Street. As you walk down look out for Pelham House Hotel signposted off the high street, and Lewes Town Hall. Approaching the river, the character of the town changes, as do the buildings. There is lots to see in this section of the town and includes many antique shops (eg., No.1 The Bridge), good places to eat such as the Real Eating Company, and Le Magasin, and a huge brewery. The latter has been in the Harvey family for over 200 years and there is a shop selling its ale, which is described as 'the champagne of beers'. Before you leave Lewes, you could visit the castle (you might need your car for this). It is open from November to

February 10am–3.45pm and from March to October 10am–5.30pm, 11am on Sundays. Further details on sussexpast.co.uk.

Charleston

This is a must. It is the former home of Bloomsbury group artists Vanessa Bell and Duncan Grant and their unconventional household. Indeed it is much more than that, because it was where some of the twentieth century's most progressive artists and writers came together to imagine society differently. As soon as they moved in (1916) Bell and Grant began to paint every surface in the farmhouse to transform it into a living piece of art. They entertained privileged bohemians, free thinkers and spirited rebels. All the liberal ideals resulted in complicated relationships.

The house, the garden, and indeed everything, is wonderful. Surprisingly, the whole estate is run by an independent charity and receives no public or government funding. It is located in Firle off the A27, 7 miles east of Lewes. The post code is BN8 6LL and it is open Wednesday to Sunday 10–5pm, but check first on charleston.org.uk.

The visits are by guided tour, which last about an hour and are absolutely fascinating. It will inspire you to learn more about the family and there is the opportunity to buy books in the shop. I recommend *Deceived with Kindness: A Bloomsbury Childhood* by Angelica Garnett who until the age of eighteen believed her father to be Vanessa's husband, Clive Bell.

There are creative workshops and events at Charleston, so it is worth looking at the website before you go, and on select Fridays an 'Extended Sisters Tour', which focuses on the relationship between Vanessa Bell and Virginia Woolf.

Monk's House

Having had you appetite whetted by visiting Charleston, Virginia Woolf and her husband Leonard's country cottage at Rodmell is lovely. It is a National Trust property in the Street, Rodmell, at

BN7 3HF and it is only open from April to October in the afternoon and must be pre-booked. It was bought in 1919 for £700 as a retreat from their hectic life in London. The 18th century weatherboard property was in a poor state when they moved in but was slowly modernised as each novel was published. It is possible to imagine Virginia's life there, writing in the morning (when her spirits were high), then getting on her bike to see her sister at Charleston in the afternoon. Their closeness is evident in many ways, including a painting on the tiles around the fireplace in Virginia's bedroom. It depicts a lighthouse, and was a present from Vanessa on the publication on *To the Lighthouse*. As you read the book, you will realise that it is almost autobiographical. It is about relationships, bereavement and family holidays. Virginia's mother died suddenly in 1895, and it is said that her father imposed his grief upon his daughters. He depended on his children (particularly his daughter Stella) to the extent they had to almost parent him. It is thought that Woolf had her first mental breakdown soon after her mother died. At the Monk's House she found happiness. It would be such a shame not to experience the place. I think of it often.

On your journey home:

Brighton

A dip into the Lanes in Brighton will give your trip a cosmopolitan finale. Once the heart of the old fishing town, this is a maze of twisting alleyways selling antiques, jewellery, gifts and more ...

The illustration is by Maria Burns from Wareham in Dorset

Swanage in Dorset

Recommended read: *The Hand of Ethelberta* by Thomas Hardy
which was written when he lived in Swanage in 1875 (or
for an easier read – one of his more well-known classics set
in Dorset)

Swanage, because of its peninsular location on the Isle of Purbeck,
has always been a bit cut-off from its surrounds. There are none of
the usual chain stores, coffee shops and restaurants that can be seen
elsewhere, so it is a special place to visit. It really feels like you are
stepping back in time (hence the choice of a Penguin Classic), yet it has
all the natural advantages of its posh neighbours – lovely sea views,
sandy beaches and its own microclimate. It is the sort of place where
you can let yourself go, because the chances that you will bump into
someone you know are pretty remote. Unfortunately one of my best
friends has an apartment there so I needed as touch of lippy 'just in
case' ... but you should be fine.

Getting there:

Wherever you are travelling from I recommend that you take the chain
ferry crossing from Sandbanks rather than driving around Poole
Harbour. The ferry operates daily and although there can be a queue at
peak times, it moves quickly, and is guaranteed to put you in the holiday
mood in the four minutes it takes to cross the harbour to Swanage.

Accommodation:

For the full Swanage experience, there really is only one place to stay,
and it is the Grand Hotel in Burlington Road, BH19 1LU
(grandhotelswanage.co.uk). It is described by the hotel as 'a classic
Victorian seaside hotel with spectacular views', and this much is true,
but with a faded charm. If you wanted somewhere truly grand (with a

price tag to match) then book into the Pig on the Beach at Studland, but you will miss the opportunity to stroll into Swanage in the evening and enjoy the pretty lights around the bay – not to mention fish and chips on the sea front.

A brief history of Swanage:

The town is first mentioned in historical texts in the Anglo-Saxon Chronicle of 877AD. It was the scene of a great naval victory by King Alfred over the Danes. Following the battle, a hundred Danish ships that had survived were driven by a terrible storm onto hard ground at Peveril Point. A small port and fishing village, Swanage flourished in the Victorian era, when quarrying of stone and marble, and then tourism, became established. In July 1833 Princess Victoria, aged fourteen, and her mother the Duchess of Kent stayed in the town, having arrived by yacht from Portsmouth. By 1885 Swanage had become a destination for the wealthy, who valued it for its fine weather, clean air and the convenience of a steam railway service direct from London. The greatest influx of visitors, however, was in 1895 when the new pier was built, bringing day-trippers to the town by paddle steamer.

Watching Punch and Judy on the beach, and looking back at the colourful beach huts lining the promenade, it is easy to imagine the town at the time. There would have been bathing machines on the water's edge, a fairground on higher ground and brass bands playing. In many ways nothing has changed. There is still a fairground, Jazz and Blues festivals in July and October, and the steam railway to Corfe is a reminder of the bygone era.

Enid Blyton loved Swanage and many of her stories were set in and around the region. In the 1950s she bought the old Isle of Purbeck Golf Club, which features in *Five Have a Mystery to Solve*. Today, children still feature as it is one of the most popular destinations for geography fieldtrips. So if you see any numbered pink pebbles on the beach, leave them where they are, or you'll disrupt the measurement of longshore drift. Not to miss when you visit:

Leave your car and stroll around the town and its seafront, exploring the little alleyways as you go. The best place for coffee is the artisan chocolatier Chococo down one of these lanes in Commercial Road. It was set up by a husband and wife team in 2002 and has grown into an award-winning ethical brand that sells in the best shops in London. Whatever you order, one small chocolate will adorn your plate.

After coffee, head up towards the high street and look out for the Mulberry Tree Gallery at number 57. This is one of the South Coast's leading independent galleries, set up by four friends 'with a passion for all things beautiful and creative'. They certainly have good taste, and you won't believe the prices. There are a string of unusual independent shops nearby so enjoy these too, as you make your way up to the town hall. The town hall's grand exterior was originally the façade of the Merciers' Hall in the City of London. It was dismantled when the road was widened, and brought to Swanage by George Burt, the owner of Purbeck House opposite. He was a wealthy stonemason who wanted to introduce a sense of civic pride in his home town, and there is a statue of him inside. Take the path to the right of the town hall to see the town's tiny prison, which has the following written above the door 'Erected for the Prevention of Vice & Immorality by the Friends of Religion & Good Order A.D. 1830'. The oldest part of Swanage is further up by the Mill Pond on Church Hill. The church of St Mary was constructed in the 13th century with the tower added a hundred years later. The date of the mill is not known but is possibly medieval, although the present mill house dates from the 18th century. This is a very peaceful enclave and the property prices in this part of Swanage reflect this.

Two places to visit before you leave Swanage itself include Peveril Point – a lovely stroll down the high street and beyond (don't miss visiting the pier to see the beautiful brass plaques screwed to the deck as you go, as mentioned in the introduction), and Durlston Country Park. For the latter you might need your car as it is a brisk thirty minute uphill walk from the centre. The address is Lighthouse Road BH19 2JL (durlston.co.uk). No explanation is needed as there is plenty of information on site – just enjoy the wonderful sea views. It is open daily from 9.30am until 5pm and there is a café in the Heritage Lottery funded Durlston Castle.

Good places to eat when you are staying in Swanage include Gee Whites for fabulous fresh fish, on the water's edge, Chilled Red in Tilly Mead (often fully booked) and the lovely Shell Bay restaurant on Ferry Road.

Tyneham Village

This is a ghost village 10 miles to the west of Swanage near Lulworth. It is only accessible when the Lulworth Ranges are open to the public see tynehamopc.org.uk. for details about visiting.

Time stopped here in 1943 when the villagers were forced to leave as the area had been chosen for forces training. Winston Churchill's War Cabinet made the decision and it is thought that D-Day preparations were made here. The villagers planned to return, but for various reasons, this never happened. Only the church and the school house remain, and even after all these years the atmosphere of abandonment is tangible. Information and photographs within the 'village' help to give a clear picture of what life was like before and after the event. As you might expect, there are no facilities at Tyneham but depending on how much time you have, it combines well with a visit to Lulworth Cove and Durdle Door.

An evening at the Rex in Wareham

Wareham is a pretty market town on the River Frome 11 miles north-east of Swanage. The car journey there is a scenic one as you pass through Corfe. In 1762, fire destroyed two-thirds of the town, which was rebuilt in Georgian architecture with red brick and Purbeck limestone; fortunately the medieval alms houses escaped unscathed. In 1914 it was a garrison town with about 7,000 soldiers living and training locally. Like Swanage, Wareham hasn't changed much, and any new development has been resisted. Edward Fox lives locally, and in 2010 campaigned against the building of a supermarket on the outskirts of the town. The town is a lovely place to visit, particularly if you stroll down to the river and pop in for a drink at the Priory (theprioryhotel.co.uk) in Church Green, but don't forget to visit the Rex in West Street – ideally returning for a film that evening (therex.co.uk).

The Rex cinema was originally the Oddfellows Hall, built in 1889, and it provided entertainment in the form of travelling theatre shows, banquets and concerts. In 1920 it became the Empire, and the 'Talkies' arrived in 1927. It has had various owners over the years but it is now a charitable trust run by enthusiastic locals. It is the people that really make it. Look out for Jocelyn Barnard in the pay box or as she emerges from behind the red curtain. She was a RADA film star in her own right, playing in *The Importance of Being Earnest* with Margaret Rutherford amongst other things, and was asked by an up-and-coming photographer to sit for him. It was Lord Snowdon. Enjoy a glass of wine as you watch your film.

The Blue Pool

Just outside Wareham at Furzebrook is a unique body of water that is either blue, green or turquoise depending on the weather. The spectrum of colour is the result of fine clay within the water, diffracting light at different angles. It is worth going a little out of your way to visit, and if you have time there is a lovely woodland walk around the pool, and the tea room is great too (bluepooltearooms.co.uk). Furzebrook Road BH20 5AR.

Corfe

The best way to visit Corfe is via the steam train from Swanage station. The castle is the hub, and is a National Trust property. Look out for the village store (Cleall's) that was given a makeover by Mary Portas years ago – unfortunately they went bankrupt soon after! The model village is a success, however, and represents what Corfe would have looked like before the destruction by Cromwell in 1646. The address is the Square, Corfe Castle, BH20 5EZ, website corfecastlemodelvillage.co.uk.

HAY-ON-WYE

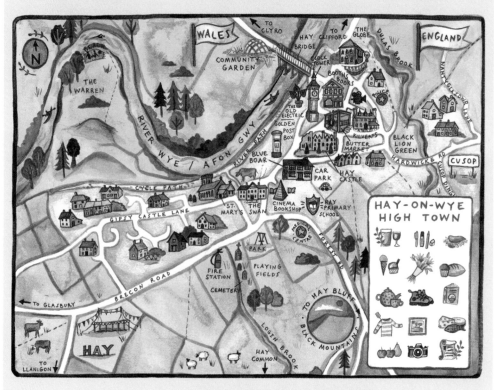

Y GELLI
POWYS, WALES

©jessicaevewatkins.com

The illustration is by Jesse Eve Watkins from the mid-Wales borderlands

Hereford and Hay-on-Wye

Recommended read: *The Red House* by Mark Haddon. Two
families. Seven days. One house. Set in Herefordshire in
2010

This trip is a lovely one and was discovered by chance. Having
decided to visit Hay-on-Wye for the book festival, I booked the
tickets in advance, but left arranging the accommodation until later,
only to find nothing was available within a wide radius of the town.
Extensive Googling threw up a monastery in Hereford where a
king-sized room with bathroom including breakfast was advertised at
an exceptionally low price. It is used mainly as a retreat (hence the
price), but if they aren't full, it is open to everyone. 'I was a stranger
and you took me in.' The rule of Saint Benedict 53.1

Accommodation:

The monastery in question is a Benedictine Abbey called Belmont and it
is in Ruckhall Lane, Hereford HR2 9RZ (belmontabbey.org.uk). The
accommodation is in Hedley Lodge (hedleylodge.com). I am sure that
they won't be offended if I tell you that it is very basic (it temporarily
closed in 2022, re-opening in January 2023, so this might not still be the
case), but the beds are comfortable and there is plenty of hot water, and
it is unbelievably peaceful. Looking out of the window you will see
monks in their brown habits walking to the abbey for regular prayer. It is
serene in the extreme.

Founded in 1859, and designed by EW Pugin, it was raised to an
abbey in 1920. There are beautiful stained-glass windows, a Hardman
altar and the daily order is observed by the resident Benedictine
community. This community is made up of about thirty monks who
follow the sixth century Rule of St Benedict, 'In all things, God may
be glorified'. In addition to welcoming visitors, they are responsible

21

for the pastoral care of parishes nearby, as well as for those as far afield as Wales, Cumbria and Peru.

Not to miss when you visit:

Hereford

Hereford on the river Wye is a cathedral city that dates back to the twelfth century. The best way to explore it is to book a Hereford guided walk. They take place daily (11.30 Monday–Saturday from around Easter to the end of October), last an hour and a half, and tickets are purchased from the cathedral shop. The website is herefordguidedwalks.org.uk. The tour will tell you everything you need to know about the town, but if the timing doesn't work, this might help: it is the county town of Herefordshire with a varied and interesting architecture, from timber-framed Jacobean buildings like the Old House Museum, to the pretty iron lacework Victorian Bridge opened in 1898 to commemorate the Diamond Jubilee of Queen Victoria. The Old House is the sole survivor of the medieval 'Butchers' Row, now furnished as it would have been in Jacobean times. On the top floor there is a model of the city as it was at the time of the Civil War. It covered 75 acres, was enclosed on one side by the river, and on the others by the city walls. The medieval buildings have been largely replaced by Georgian brick terraces.

The cathedral has been here since the city was founded. Most of the present building dates from the twelfth century, but the central tower and choir stalls were constructed 200 years later. The cathedral contains some of the finest examples of Normal architecture up to the present day, including the thirteenth century shrine of St Thomas of Hereford. The cathedral is dedicated to St Mary and St Ethelbert, a king of East Anglia who was murdered near Hereford in AD 794. His tomb became a famous shrine in the Middle Ages. Moreover, the cathedral precincts house the famous Mappa Mundi, a world map drawn on vellum around AD 1300, which shows the world as flat, with Jerusalem at the centre. It also has King Stephen's 800-year-old chair, and a large chained library containing over 1,500 ancient books.

After visiting the cathedral (or your tour) stroll around the town focusing particularly on older part of the city located around the cathedral and near the bridge. Here you will find small independent shops selling local cheeses, handmade silver jewellery and luxury clothing. The best places to eat can be found here too. The town itself has stayed true to its trading-centre past and it is very much a market town with cider, Hereford beef and leather goods being top of the list.

Ross-on-Wye and Bridstow

A drive to Ross-on-Wye from your Hereford base is well worth doing if only for the views. St Mary's Church spire has shaped the skyline for over 700 years, but the scenery across the whole part of this southern section of Herefordshire is lovely. It is great walking country and there are trails of different lengths circumnavigating the region. For more information see the visitherefordshire.co.uk site and look for the Wye Tours.

Like Hereford, Ross-on-Wye is independently minded, and it was just outside the town that I discovered the Japanese-inspired store that is mentioned in the introduction. Baileys is described as a 'home store', but it is so much more and really wonderful. Neither the website, baileyshome.co.uk, or the reviews, do it justice. It has won awards and is to be found at Whitecross Farm, Bridstow, Ross-on-Wye, HR9 6JU. It is run by Mark and Sally Bailey and they are the masters of quality. They choose simple, useful and beautiful items, and display them in an innovative way. Perfection in the form of imperfection (wabi-sabi) runs throughout; from the display cases, to the counters, to the garden café where the freshly made produce were in a league of their own. Definitely don't miss having something to eat and drink in the café. Everything in the store is sourced locally; from a man that makes wooden dibbers, to a potter who throws traditional deep clay pots, to a local blacksmith who makes sturdy door handles (that you can hardly bear to remove your hand from they are so tactile). I bought a reading lamp that clamps onto a desk and every time I see it I admire it.

A night at the monastery followed by Baileys will feed the soul of anyone but the most stonyhearted. Hopefully you will be well rested for a longish drive the next day.

Hay-on-Wye

Even if you don't take this trip whilst the book festival is on (though I suggest you do), Hay-on-Wye is well worth a visit. It is a compact entity with bookshops, vintage boutiques and an ice cream parlour – all within a stroll of one another. Look out for the most adorable mini Tintin models balancing on display shelves in the most unlikely places. The town itself has just 2,000 residents but this swells to about 100,000 in the festival week, though it doesn't seem to diminish the enjoyment as the town effectively gears itself up for the invasion. There is a lot to do and see whilst in the vicinity, from exploring Hay's Jacobean castle with its honesty bookshop, to canoeing down the river, to walking the water meadow that is known as the Warren and is accessed via a path alongside St Mary's Church.

If you have organised to visit the book festival, a shuttle bus takes you from the town to the tented village. There is a sense of excitement as you enter and it is possible to pick up tickets from a returns/swap board near the gate. I suggest looking out for the more controversial speakers. I went to a talk by Oliver James titled 'The real reason children are like their parents' and it caused disquiet in the audience as his belief that patterns of nurture are the key to everything regardless (almost) of genetics wasn't well received at all. His book Upping Your Ziggy is based on a comparison of David Bowie with his psychotic brother Terry. All the authors sign copies of their books in the book shop tent on site – his wasn't a long queue!

En route between Hereford and Hay-on-Wye is the 'Black & White' Villages Trail. Ancient villages with pretty timber-framed buildings. Weobley, for example, was once famed for wool making, then gloves and subsequently ale, and it is where Charles I stayed overnight during the Civil War. A map can be downloaded from visitherefordshire.co.uk.

On your journey home, if you have time:

Berrington Hall

About 25 miles north of Hereford is the National Trust property of Berrington Hall (berrington@nationaltrust.org.uk) Telephone 01568 615721. It is the perfect house in the perfect setting. Indeed it is described by the Trust as Georgian grandeur on a human scale; a neoclassical mansion by Henry Holland set in 'Capability' Brown's final landscape and gardens. Opening times vary but in the spring and summer it is open daily from 11am.

From the exterior it looks rather austere with its red sandstone façade, but inside it is amazing with Biagga Rebecca ceilings, period furniture and an unfolding story of Ann Bangham, the first lady of Berrington. Equally interesting are the servants' quarters; they were designed to enable movement around the house unseen by the family and guests.

Don't leave without seeing the walled garden.

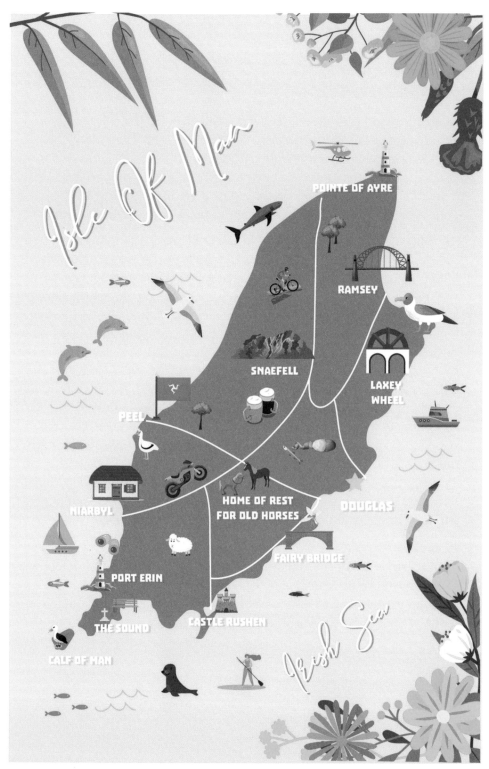

The illustration is by Lucy Judge

The Isle of Man

Recommended read: *The Particular Appeal of Gillian Pugsley* by
Susan Ornbratti, a love story and a discovery on the
Isle of Man

This trip is one of the longest in the book and, depending on where you are travelling from, includes a night in Liverpool. The Isle of Man is the perfect place to visit because it is just 33 miles by 13 miles in size, and has a very different feel to the rest of the United Kingdom. It is a 'crown dependency' with its own parliament, traditions, currency and the Manx dialect. Most organised trips to the island focus on the railways, of which there are three; the Steam Railway, Manx Electric Railway and the Snaefell Mountain Railway. Visitors can buy an inclusive ticket that allows unlimited travel on these and the horse-drawn trams on Douglas's promenade. On my visit, I started by going to some of the recommended guide book destinations, but became quite disillusioned very quickly (don't, for example, rush to visit Erin's Art Centre, allocate much time to seeing the Laxey Wheel, or go out of your way to shop at Tynwald Mills), but do visit the parliament building Tynwald at Finch Road in Douglas, spend a bit of time in Castletown as you drive south, and look briefly at Ramsey when you visit Milntown Estate.

I found many of the best places to visit were found through adverts in the local paper. Indeed, the island has a knack of keeping things quiet and this was true in so many ways. Parking on the island, for example, is enabled by putting a timed dial (with no instructions) on your dashboard and these are available free (on an unmarked shelf) on the ferry.

Getting there:

Unless you fly and hire a car, the best way to get to the island is via the Steam Packet Ferry Company. It takes 2hrs 45mins from Liverpool and you need to be ready to drive on about an hour before. It is an easy and pleasant experience with food and films on board. If booked in advance it isn't too expensive. I took the 11.15am crossing on a Thursday in July from Liverpool, returning on the 7.30am from Douglas four days later. There is a 3pm crossing but do check dates and times as they vary through the year. Sailings also take place from Heysham, Birkenhead, Dublin and Belfast. NB Take care to avoid visiting the island during the motorcycle races, the biggest being the Tourist Trophy in May/June.

Accommodation:

If travelling far, I suggest booking one night at the Atlantic Tower Hotel in Liverpool for the evening before. It is ideal in that it is located minutes from the Mersey tunnel, has its own parking, and directly overlooks the Steam Packet terminal. It is also opposite the grade 1 listed Royal Liver Building and is walking distance from everything. I saw many of Liverpool's highlights in the short time that I was there, partly because the city is a collection on 'quarters' so it is easy to find places of interest all close together. In the heritage quarter, for example, is the Anglican cathedral described by John Betjeman as 'one of the greatest buildings in the world', and in the arts quarter the £70m contemporary National Museum designed by a Danish architect, and clad in spectacular folded limestone. Next door is the award-winning Beatles Story with the even more impressive brass statue of the four of them outside. Look at the swing in their feet to see how it is brought to life.

My recommendation for the Isle of Man is the Claremont Hotel in Douglas at 18 Loch Promenade, IM1 2LX (claremonthoteldouglas. com). It is a three-storey townhouse on the seafront. It is the highest rated hotel on the island with four-star status, and it is minutes from the Steam Packet Ferry terminal. The décor sets it apart from anything else on the island, with a lovely mix of contemporary furnishings alongside wonderful vintage travel posters. Booked via a portal like Trivago or Booking.com it is possible to stay here for a similar price to a much less stylish hotel nearby. The Isle of Man – despite its tax haven status – isn't wealthy, so everything is sensibly priced. If you just book bed and breakfast at the hotel, there is the opportunity to visit some really good restaurants nearby like 14 North, and the Little Fish Café in North Quay, and/or Macfarlane's, which is a stroll away in Duke Street. All are good value. But if you are feeling strapped for cash, I had the best freshly cooked pizza in years from Domino's on the seafront followed by an ice cream in Davisons opposite the tram stop.

More about the island:

Legend has it that the Isle of Man was created when the Irish giant Finn MacCooill threw a chunk of earth from Ireland's coastline towards Scotland, which then landed in the Irish Sea and became the Isle of Man. The symbol of the island is the three legs of Man representing 'whichever way you throw me I stand'. The island is proud of its independence and its varied history, particularly the fact that the Romans probably never invaded but the Vikings did, more than 1,000 years ago. There is a replica Viking ship in the House of Mannannan in Peel. This museum provides a detailed history of the island, a brief summary of which is as follows:

After a period during which the Kingdom of Mann passed between English and Scottish rule, in 1333 Edward III renounced English claims and recognised it as an independent kingdom, but in 1399 the island's king, William, was executed for treason by Henry IV and the Isle of Man passed back to the English crown. In 1405 the kingdom was given to Sir John Stanley, whose descendants held it for 360 years before the 1765 Isle of Man Purchase Act returned it to British Crown.

The island was used by the British Government for the internment of enemy aliens (subjects of a foreign nation with which the government was in conflict) during the World Wars. There were two large camps on the island, at Douglas and Knockaloe near Peel. The first was a requisitioned holiday camp, whilst the second was purpose built using prefabricated huts and had its own railway. There are fascinating photographs relating to this period on Douglas's promenade with a focus on enemy aliens. On the outbreak of WWII there were about 80,000 potential enemy aliens in Britain who, it was feared, could be spies, or willing to assist Britain's enemies in the event of invasion. All Germans and Austrians over sixteen were called before special tribunals and were divided into three groups: 'A' high security (about 600), who were immediately interned and sent to camps like these; 'B' doubtful cases (around 6,500), who were supervised and subject to restrictions; and 'C' no risk. (Source bbc.co.uk Civilian Internment 1939–1945).

Do look out for a Manx cat when you are there. It is virtually tailless as a result of a naturally occurring mutation and a dominant gene; and of note, plenty of famous people were born on the island, including the late-Victorian scholar Thomas Edward Brown, the comedian Norman Wisdom, the Bee Gees and the cyclist Mark Cavendish.

There is lots to see and do on the island, but try not to miss the following:

Cregneash Folk Museum and the Sound

A lovely morning's visit (to the south of the island) consists of the following: coffee overlooking Chapel Bay at Port St Mary, a stroll around the folk museum, and lunch at the Sound café.

Port St Mary is full of local families, has a relaxed coffee shop and looks out over a sweeping horseshoe-shaped bay.

A short drive up into the hills takes you to Cregneash with its wonderful rural life centre. Take your National Trust card if you have one (although they won't think to ask for it!) and you can get to see everything for free. The visit starts with a short film about the life of a crofter and then you are directed around the tiny cottage that houses the shop and café. The best bit was going inside the furnished buildings, two of which had guides in traditional dress … each described a typical day. I got the feeling that it rarely gets very busy so it is a peaceful retreat where it is possible to fully appreciate how hard life was in the nineteenth century. Scenes from the film Waking Ned were filmed in and around Cregneash, although it was supposed to have been set in an Irish village. The museum is open daily from 25th March until 30th October from 10am. Cregneash Road IM9 5PX (manxnationalheritage.im).

To get to the Sound just continue past the museum on a road that looks like it is going nowhere. It is no distance – you could almost walk, but there is a car park at your destination. The view will take your breath away. This is one of the most picturesque points in the south and overlooks water to the small island called the Calf of Man. It is a natural paradise, and you will likely see a seal. The café has a 180 degree view through a curved glass window. It is open 10am–9pm daily from April until October, and 10am–4pm in November to March. Sound Road IM9 5PZ (visitisleofman.com).

The House of Manannan to the west of the island, at Peel

Peel gets mentioned quite a lot in the guide books because it is one of the oldest cathedral cities in the British Isles, dating back to the sixth century, so I was looking forward to visiting. Unfortunately they were digging up the car park when I arrived so it wasn't looking its best. However, if you look beyond such things (and the plethora of dimly lit barber shops that seem to be everywhere on the island), then you will see narrow winding colourful streets, and get a sense that you have stepped back in time. Head for the renovated waterfront where there are smarter coffee shops, small restaurants and an art gallery. From here you can see Peel Castle standing on St Patrick's Isle, which is connected to the town by a causeway and can be visited daytime from the end of May until October.

Peel was a major fishing port in its heyday, and remains the most active fishing centre on the island. In peak summer there are two water related activities in the harbour, the annual Viking Longboat Race whereby teams of ten rowers, many in Viking gear, race against each other, and the Peel Traditional Boat weekend where teams of four build a boat using materials supplied within a set time, and the most sail-worthy 'boat' wins. The House of Mannanan gets mixed reviews on trip adviser, but I thought it was great. It uses multimedia to tell the islands story with short film clips, talking waterfalls and realistic room sets. In one such room you can choose whose story you want to hear and for once women get a good look in. Press the button for a seafarer's wife to realise that it isn't so bad being a golf widow after all! The period of history post 1300 gets a bit laborious, so just read the summary above and you'll get the gist. The museum is open daily 10am until 5pm throughout the year with few exceptions. Mill Road, IM5 1TA (manxnationalhertigate.im).

Milntown Estate to the north of the island near Ramsey

This really is a best kept secret, and is only open for tours on Wednesdays and Saturdays at 2.30pm, so plan your visit accordingly, ideally by booking in advance on 01624 818091. There are three good reasons to go; the house, the garden and the fantastic café (full of locals because visitors have been kept completely in the dark about it). The house is in a 'wedding cake' style which was a common feature of Manx architecture during the Regency period. It has a bit of everything from a classical Italianate entrance hall, to a 'strawberry gothic' library, to elements of a 1770s farmhouse in the bedrooms. It has also been lots of things since the early sixteenth century, from the home of the Christian family, a school, a hotel and then a family home again for Charles Peel Yates (of Yates' Wine Lodges) and latterly the Edwards family. Sir Clive Edwards moved to Milntown in 1963 with his mother Lady Kathleen Edwards and his lifetime friend Bob Thomas. The estate was bequeathed by him to the people of the Isle of Man in 1999. What I found interesting when taking the 2.30pm guided tour was that everything is exactly as Clive Edwards left it, and there were 'no holds barred' in showing us its contents, including folded pyjamas in the dresser, Bob Thomas's vintage motorcycle inspired bedroom, and their collection of Rupert Bears. It was almost too personal, but unique as a result.

The gardens surround the house and cover 15 acres of garden and woodland. There are dazzling displays of rhododendrons, magnolias, and camellias from early spring to summer. The herbaceous borders and kitchen garden look good throughout the year, as does the walled garden. The café is set in a conservatory and has lovely views. The food and presentation was similar to what you might expect in a London bistro, quite unusual for its location just outside Ramsey. New to the estate is accommodation in the form of three self-catering apartments each with two double rooms. The café at Milntown is open daily from 10am (except Tuesday), the gardens the same but just between 8th February and 30th October, and the house 2.30pm on Wednesday and Saturday from 30th March to 28th September. Milntown, Lezayre, IM7 2AB (milntown.org).

The illustration is by Sophie Hodges of Inky Acorn Designs

Whitstable in Kent

Recommended read: *The Whitstable Pearl Mystery* by Julie Wassmer, her debut mystery novel

If you've not been to Whitstable before, you are in for a treat. It is quirky, bracing and atmospheric – with amazing seafood. The suggestion is you go with a friend (for a minimum of two nights) and visit Margate and Faversham as well.

Accommodation:

The recommendation for this trip is to stay in a 150-year-old converted fisherman's hut located on the beach, in the centre of Whitstable. These huts are colourful wooden structures that have been converted into good quality (but not hugely expensive) overnight accommodation with breakfast being taken at the nearby Art Deco Hotel Continental. Despite the low ceilings, they are light and airy and it feels and sounds like you are sleeping on a boat. The website is whitstablefishermanshuts.com and the address of the hotel where you book and collect your key is 29 Beach Walk, CT5 2BP. It is a bit tricky to find so you'll need the postcode.

Whitstable

Whitstable and its neighbour Margate have spearheaded the revitalisation of the British seaside resorts. Gone are the donkey rides and mini-golf (phew to the latter) and in have come the multi-million pound investments in the arts with the Turner Contemporary Gallery in Margate and the Horsebridge Gallery in Whitstable. It has always been arty, independent and special. Turner painted it, Somerset Maugham wrote about it and holiday makers from the East End of London came in their droves to enjoy oysters from Wheelers on the high street (now the Whitstable Oyster Company). Although more 'posh', it hasn't changed much. It is impossible to visit Whitstable without feeling its history, much of which relates to the sea. The Romans discovered its oysters and shipped them back to Rome (alive). In 1480 Whitstable acquired its first fish market in St Margaret's Street, and in 1830 the 'Crab and Winkle Line' (properly known as the Canterbury and Whitstable Railway) was opened. It was the world's first steam-hauled passenger railway and in 1832 the company opened up the harbour to enable passengers to go to London from the port. The line closed in 1953, but is now a footpath and cycleway. The town oozes character with narrow higgledy piggledy streets and weatherboard cottages, particularly along Island Wall. The high street is full of independent shops, including a cheese maker and the Wine Room. It is just a case of strolling round the town and seafront to absorb the character.

Not to miss when you've had your fill of Whitstable:

Margate

Described as having the 'loveliest skies in all Europe' it has so much more. It is best to focus on the far end of Margate near the old town and try to fit a walk in:

The Viking Coastal Trail is a scenic traffic-free coastal path that takes you east of Margate to Broadstairs (on foot or by bike), a distance of about 8 km. It is signposted on the higher ground behind the Turner Contemporary, and is an easy walk all the way. There is an interesting stopping point close to Broadstairs at Bleak House. This is the nineteenth century mansion that Charles Dickens rented to write David Copperfield. It is now a hotel, located in Fort Road, post code BN8 6LL. It is advisable to contact them beforehand to book either for tea, a short tour, or indeed just to check they are still open post-pandemic. Visit bleakhousebroadstairs.co.uk or telephone 01834 865338. To return from Broadstairs to Margate take bus number 56.

The Turner Contemporary also has a history. Turner's landlady when he stayed here was Mrs Booth. She has been immortalised in shells at the far end of the promenade, and the gallery itself has been built on her home. The gallery is free to visit and is open Tuesday–Sunday 10am–5pm and has a café as well as an excellent shop. Here you can pick up a 'Tracy Emin', a collection of white ceramics featuring small and detailed drawings from this local artist (turnercontemporary.org).

The old town of Margate: Linking with the statue of Mrs Booth on the seafront, the old town has its own shell grotto. It was discovered in 1835 when James Newlove lowered his son into a hole in the ground that had appeared during the digging of a duck pond. The boy emerged describing tunnels covered with shells. It came as a complete surprise to the people of Margate and debate has raged about its origins ever since. Sceptical of anything with the word 'grotto' in the title (reminiscent of downmarket pop-ups), I was pleasantly surprised. Apparently there are 4.6 million shells and the mosaic is beautiful. Unfortunately the grotto is only open at the weekends (and some school holidays). It can be found by walking down King Street then turning left into Grotto Hill. The phone number is 01843 220008 and the website shellgrotto.co.uk. To get to the shell grotto via King Street you will walk past the Tudor House. This is one of the oldest surviving buildings in Margate and is typical of the period with a timber frame and construction techniques popular in the fifteenth century. It also has limited opening times: Wednesday, Saturday and Sunday 11.30am–2.30pm and bank holidays. It is possible to buy a combined ticket for the Margate Museum and the Tudor House by ringing 01843 231213 or popping into the museum whilst you're there. What I particularly enjoyed on my visit to Margate's old town visit was exploring the numerous antique and old-style homeware shops that abound in this part of the town. I will single out just one and it is called 1 Duke Street. Do visit if you can. For tea I visited the Seaside Cake Parlour in Hawley Street (en route to the Tudor House), there is an amazing selection of homemade cakes and not in huge portions either. If you go, look out for a book on their shelf called 'Cake Wrecks' it is very funny. The cake on the cover shows a professionally made cake with the wording … 'Best wishes Suzanne, Under Neat that, We will miss you'.

Faversham

To the south-west of Whitstable, about a 20-minute drive away is the medieval town of Faversham. It is truly lovely. It is the only town in the UK to use the royal arms of England as its own. There are nearly 500 listed buildings in the town. Some are Georgian, a few Victorian, one or two later. At least half are either medieval or Elizabethan. The heart of the town is cobbled and it is not surprising that it is regularly used as a film location. The best way to see the town is to pop into the visitor information centre at 10 Preston Street and pick up the Faversham Town History Trail, which highlights ten places of interest including Standard Quay.

On your journey home if you have time:

Chartwell

Chances are that wherever you live, the best route home will be via the M25, and Chartwell is located off junction 5/6 not far off the A25. It is not much more than a couple of miles south of Westerham and the address is Mapleton Road, TN16 1PS. This National Trust property was the place that truly inspired Sir Winston Churchill (less so his wife – see below) and it is where he developed his artistic talents, focusing particularly on the lake. The house has been left very much as it was when the family lived here with pictures, books, and personal mementoes. Entry to the house is by timed ticket 11am–5pm from the end of February until the end of October, and the gardens, shop and café are open throughout the year. Visit chartwell@nationaltrust.org.uk.

Following your visit you might be interested to read *Clementine Churchill* by their daughter Mary Soames. Of Chartwell for Winston she wrote, 'Chartwell never failed him in good times and bad. Not even in the last sad years when, silent and remote from us all, he would sit for hours in the golden sunshine of the summer days, gazing out over his enchanted valley and lakes; down over the lushly green and tufted Wealden landscape beyond, which melts at last into the faint blue-grey line of the South Downs.'

Of Chartwell for Clementine she wrote, 'The house frankly appalled her. It was a grey Victorian mansion, built round, and on the site of a much older house; hemmed in by noisome laurels, it was damp, dreary and ugly.' She did 'come round' eventually, but she never loved it like he did.

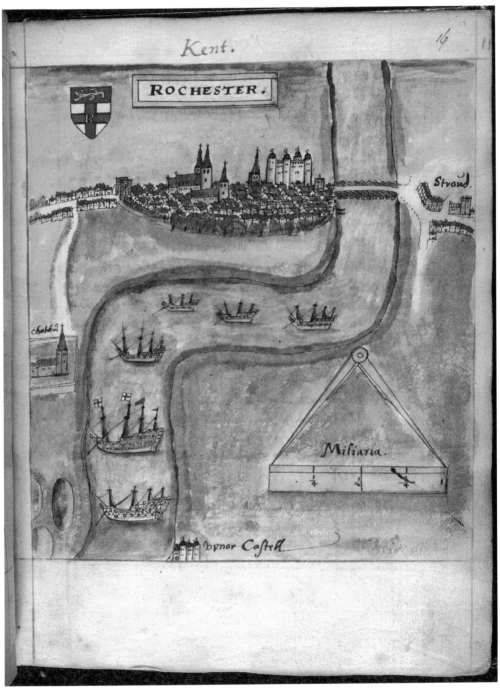

The illustration dates back to 1588 and is by permission of The British Library

Rochester in Kent

Choose a second-hand book from Baggins Bazaar at
19 High Street

This very short trip is linked to the previous one in that it relates to Charles Dickens, but with the historic Chatham (and an outlet centre) thrown in.

Accommodation:

The recommended place to stay is the Ship & Trades hotel on St Mary's Island in Chatham. It is a former dockyard office and engineering shop that dates back to 1875. It has recently been refurbished and is tastefully decorated in a style appropriate to its marina setting. Travelling alone, I booked a single room via Trivago and was allocated a fabulous double room with a great bath, and views of the river Medway. The website is shipandtradeschatham .co.uk and the address Maritime Way, Chatham Maritime, ME4 3ER.

Chatham

The hotel is just a stone's throw from the historic dockyard (thedockyard.co.uk) so depending on your arrival time, this is a good starting point. No ticket is needed to enter the discovery centre, which gives a basic flavour of the place, but to go inside the three historic warships that are housed there (*HMS Gannet, Cavalier* and *HM Submarine Ocelot*), and to take the Victorian ropery tour etc. means allocating quite a bit of time and buying an all-inclusive ticket, albeit valid for a year. Walking back, via the water, I stumbled upon an outlet centre. I wouldn't normally recommend such places, but needing so many outfits for golf club events, it is quite handy to be able to buy a pair of shoes for less than half the price elsewhere. It is called the Quays, just look out for the Range and Cadbury's, close to the hotel. In the evening

41

the centre (around Pier 5) comes alive as there are restaurants everywhere. The best is probably an Italian called Villagio, the worst an 'all you can eat', the Real China. I went to Zippers, which was very relaxed, and you don't feel self-conscious eating alone as you look out over the water. Other choices include Wok to Go where you can design your own rice or noodle stir fry, and an ice cream parlour.

Rochester

Having carried out a reconnoitre the afternoon before, I returned for the full experience the following day. Rochester exudes history. Forgetting for now its cathedral (8), and the twelfth century castle (9), both of which deserve time for discovery, the high street is the real gem. So my recommendation is that you visit the visitors centre in the middle of the town and purchase the 'In Dickens' Footsteps' town trail. If they are out of stock, it can be downloaded easily (and for free) online. It includes a map of Rochester with notes alongside. The start is the Guildhall Museum (12), at the top of the street and then it takes you to see the following key buildings:

The Corn Exchange (13) was built in 1706 and can't be missed because of its large projecting clock. Dickens first encountered the clock as a boy when walking with his father and it featured in *The Uncommercial Traveller*.

The Six Poor Travellers' House (1), was founded by Richard Watts (MP for Rochester in 1563) as a charity for six poor travellers to receive a night's free lodging. Dickens was an advocate of social reform and the means of achieving this he believed was by philanthropy and education. In one of his short stories 'The Seven Poor Travellers' Dickens became the seventh traveller and describes his arrival at this very door.

Restoration House (5), is located down Crow Lane opposite the Vines. It is an Elizabethan red-brick mansion that was renamed 'Satis House' by Dickens in *Great Expectations* as the home of Miss Havisham. It was built in 1587 and it is said that Charles II stayed here on 28th May 1660 at his restoration. It is open to the public from June to September, 10am to 5pm.

The Vines Park (6), is over the road from Restoration House, and was formerly the priory vineyard of Rochester Cathedral. It was featured in *The Mystery of Edwin Drood*. It was a meadow in Dickens' time and he was seen leaning against a fence just two days before he died.

Eastgate House and Dickens' Chalet (3 and 2), are back on the high street opposite number 150. Eastgate House is also Elizabethan and built about the same time as Restoration House. It appears in *The Mystery of Edwin Drood* as the Nuns' House, a school for young ladies (which it was in Dickens' time). Partly hidden alongside is a Swiss chalet given to Dickens by Charles Fletcher, a French actor friend, and used as his adored study. It has been moved here from Gad's Hill Place where it was delivered to Dickens in fifty-eight packing cases.

150 High Street (4), is divided into three separate premises when originally it was one timber-framed mansion built in 1684. It features in *Great Expectations* as Mr Pumblechook's house, where he carried on business as a corn chandler, and again in *The Mystery of Edwin Drood* as the offices of Mr Sapsea, an auctioneer.

At (7) is a row of eighteenth century houses, at (14) Jasper's Gatehouse and Mr Topes' House. Dickens described these two as if they were one in, linked together by a connecting door. Finally (11) is the Royal Victoria and Bull Hotel. In *The Pickwick Papers* Dickens used the real name of the Bull Hotel and indeed stayed there himself. It acquired the prefix 'Royal Victoria' following an overnight stop by Princess Victoria in 1836.

If you plan to complete Dickens' life in Rochester, there are two final stops for which you will need your car. The first is number 2 Ordnance Terrace, where he came to live with his family aged four in 1816, and the second Gad's Hill Place at Higham ME3 7PA. The second is a grade 1 listed eighteenth century house and was Dickens' final home. It is now a school but it is open one weekend a month for afternoon tea. It is booked by ringing Towncentric in Gravesend on 01474 337600. It is worth going even if you can't get in for tea because it is where Dickens achieved his boyhood ambition. It was when out walking with his father that he saw it and thought it 'the most beautiful house ever seen'. Noting his son's fascination, his father used to say to him that 'if ever you grow up to be a clever man perhaps you might own that house ...'

Rochester Cathedral

Rochester Cathedral is England's second oldest, having been founded in AD 604 by Bishop Justus. The present building dates back to the work of the French monk Bishop Gundulf in 1083. Look out for the magnificent fourteenth century Chapter Library door.

The cathedral became a major place of pilgrimage in the thirteenth century, following the death of William of Perth, a Scottish baker who was murdered nearby. His body was brought to the cathedral and at his shrine it is said that miracles were performed. Modern pilgrims who journey to the cathedral still climb the Pilgrim Steps, now worn by the many thousands of medieval pilgrims visiting the shrine, often lighting candles at the William of Perth prayer-station in front of the oratory.

Rochester Castle

This is looked after by English Heritage and is open Tuesday to Sundays with no requirement to book. The main tower-keep was built around 1127 by William of Corbeil, Archbishop of Canterbury, with the encouragement of Henry I. It consists of three floors with a set of defences in place – prior to entry at first floor level. In 1215, garrisoned by rebel barons, the castle endured an epic siege by King John. Having first undermined the outer wall, John used the fat of forty pigs to fire a mine under the keep, bringing its southern corner crashing down. Even then the defenders held on, until they were eventually starved out after resisting for two months.

Rebuilt under Henry III and Edward I, the castle remained as a viable fortress until the sixteenth century.

On your journey home:

Owletts

This is a National Trust property, 1.3 km to the northwest of Cobham near Gravesend at the Street, DA12 3AP. It is a red-brick Charles II house with a lovely garden. It is an example of a Kent country home with architectural influences of its most famous owner, Sir Herbert Baker. It is only open on Sundays 11am–5pm April to September and has been recently closed, so do check on nationaltrust.org.uk before you go. Email: owletts@nationaltrust.org.uk.

LEIGHTON MOSS

HORNBY CASTLE

MORECAMBE

HEYSHAM

LANCASTER

TROUGH OF BOWLAND

PENDLE

N
W E
S

BEACON FELL

CLITHEROE

BLACKPOOL

PRESTON

BLACKBURN

BURNLEY

ACCRINGTON

LYTHAM ST. ANNES

E.WAREING
TARLETON

LEYLAND

DARWEN

ORMSKIRK

SARSAPARILLA
WINE

RAWTENSTALL

CHORLEY

TURTON

◆ LANCASHIRE ◆

The illustration is by Bek Cruddace. Lancashire is her home county.

Lytham St Annes in Lancashire

Recommended read: *Owl Song at Dawn* by Emma Claire
Sweeny, a fabulous and unusual book set in Morecambe.
Do read it.

This short trip is located in the vicinity of the well-known Royal Lytham Golf Course, which was formed in 1886 – so in theory – you could visit with your golfing partner. Two nights are best, and it is all about absorbing the atmosphere rather than dashing here, there and everywhere.

Accommodation:

I went on my own and stayed at the Grand on the promenade. I know the area well because my grandparents lived there. The Grand has gone up and down over the years (being in competition with the Clifton Arms in Lytham just down the road) but it has finally found its feet after a major refurbishment and is very good indeed. There is a contemporary annex a couple of doors down called Grand TwentyTwo, and because there are often more spare rooms than people, you can usually get a good deal by booking direct. They have a new manager who is very 'hands on', so standards remain consistently high, and talking of hands, look out for the receptionist who has the most beautiful nails. The website is the-grand.co.uk and the address South Promenade, Lytham St Annes, FY8 1NB. Telephone 01253 643424.

I visit quite regularly, and each time enjoy the contrast between Lytham to the south-east, Blackpool to the north, with St Annes balanced in between. Rather than rush round trying to see and do everything, I like to live like a native and pop into the public library (just around the corner from the Grand), sit on the top deck of the number 7 bus, and eat out where the locals go – but otherwise it is always good with a book, in the hotel.

A bit of history:

In 1922 the town towns of Lytham and St Annes-on-the-Sea were merged to form the Borough of Lytham St Annes. The birth of both closely relates to local wealthy families, particularly Colonel Clifton, the Squire of Lytham. He wanted to develop the 'West End' that would become St Annes. All there was in 1870 – apart from the dunes – was a railway from Blackpool to Lytham, a lighthouse and several farms and cottages that paid rent to the Clifton estate. He considered the dunes 'a blank canvas', and in 1872 started to build a road parallel to the sea called Clifton Drive and then by another St Annes Road named after the new parish church.

A significant name thereafter was Elijah Hargreaves. He had made his fortune in the cotton industry and was visiting Blackpool – walking on the dunes – when he saw what was happening and realised the huge potential. In 1874 he formed the St Annes Land & Building Company, and leased land from Colonel Clifton in what was to become the centre of the town. Other companies joined soon after, to provide the services the new town needed. Plans were drawn, builders' huts appeared and the building began. Finally another cotton merchant, William Porritt, invested a further £250,000 into the town to give it the character it still has today. In 1910 the Majestic Hotel was built between the pier and St Annes Square. It had 200 bedrooms, tennis courts and was the height of luxury. Stars performing in Blackpool shows in the 1920s stayed there. It was considered one of St Annes' finest treasures but was sadly demolished in 1975 due to prohibitive running costs. It was replaced by five-storey flats.

Lytham

It seems that whatever is happening in the UK and beyond, Lytham stays untouched. It has such a strong identity; it just keeps going whatever. There is the timeless Stringers department store (St Annes equivalent JR Taylors unfortunately bit the dust a while ago), the dress shop 'Poppy', where they have things you have been imagining for years but never been able to find, and independent coffee shop after coffee shop that are rarely empty. Strolling along the front towards the windmill you will see lovely period properties, breathe in the salty sea air and be welcomed in to pop-up exhibitions in the old swimming baths. Do look at the war memorial and gardens by the clock, and then if you have your car, I strongly suggest you visit Lytham Hall – Lancashire's Downton Abbey. It is an eighteenth century country house in 78 acres of parkland just 1 mile from the town centre, and it is where the Squire of Lytham Colonel Clifton – as mentioned previously – lived. It has been the subject of a £5 million fundraising campaign, and you will meet the colourful characters that have shaped the history of the place. There are guided tours of the house (albeit not daily) and a really good tea room. Visit: lythamhall.org.uk or phone 01253 736652, email:Lytham.hall@htnw. co.uk, and whilst there buy the guide book *Harry Clifton Squire of Lytham* by Peter Watson. Described as 'The extraordinary life of an English eccentric', it will tell you everything you need to know – and more, about the rise and fall of the Squire of Lytham.

Finally, whilst you are in Lytham, walk down to Fairhaven Lake, which is en route to Swanage where there is crazy golf and pedalos, and look up what is playing at Lowther Gardens Theatre. I am rarely disappointed by their productions (lowtherpavilion.co.uk).

St Annes

Home of the late Les Dawson, whose statue is on St Annes promenade.

St Annes got its name through the commissioning of the parish church by Lady Clifton. It was in the early 1870s and she named it in memory of her aunt, Anne. The town has its own charm and character with a laid-back approach to life. Once you have strolled around the town the two places to visit are the pier and Ashton Gardens. The pier was built in 1885 as a sedate promenading venue for the resort's visitors. Attractions were added later, but they haven't detracted from this grade 2 listed building. The gardens are also listed and include a Japanese, rose and rock garden. The gardens were originally established in 1874 as St George's Gardens, then in 1914 there was a competition to redesign them, which was won by a local man, Mr F. Harrison. He incorporated more diversity but still kept the undulating character, reflecting the topography of the area. The gardens underwent a major refurbishment in 2010 when it received £1,436,000 in lottery funding.

Before you move on, do look and listen. The red brick of the town, the old chimneys, the down to earth attitude of the people. They are sensible to the core. Not much more than a generation ago the mills were where the residents of the town worked. The long hours, the noise, the poor pay has all fed into their appreciation of the here and now. They stand firm on their values and attitudes. One of the reasons I loved the recommended read was the main character – 80-year old Maeve, is a true Lancashire stalwart ... on page 54 she is told the world needs more people like her (which it does), yet her response was 'There was no one I despised more than do-gooders'.

Blackpool

Because Blackpool hasn't had the best reputation – with its penchant for hen and stag parties parading down the golden mile – the temptation is to bypass it and focus on the surrounds. This, however, is a mistake, because it is in the process of a major revamp. The background to Blackpool is well known. Described by JB Priestley as a pleasure resort without exclusiveness, 'indeed they decided to make a move in the opposite direction. They would turn it into a pleasure resort for the crowds.' That crowd was the Lancashire cotton mill workers. Wonderful holidays were had by those with very little but a desire to enjoy themselves: 'More often than not, they paid for their lodgings on arrival, for then they knew that every penny left could be spent; and they returned home with a stick or two of rock, a plush-framed photograph of the Tower and the Wheel, the other half of their excursion ticket, and nothing else.'

The start of the downward slide in Blackpool's fortunes was twofold. Firstly other resorts started to match what they did best, hence numbers dwindled, and secondly they gave up on originality. The amusements became more serious and Americanised. To try and win back its former clientele it copied what its rivals were offering and the move to mediocrity took hold. It is reinventing itself as a 'grown up museum with a sense of fun' and as the host of the British National Dance Championships it has definitely started to put itself back on the map. The promenade has been widened and lovely 30m tall giant 'blades of grass' sculptures sway in the wind. Where there were grotty burger bars now stands the Beach House Café and Bar with a swish new tourist information office next door. It is still a long way off getting everything right (free entry to stroll around the inside of Blackpool Tower is only known about by the locals, so visitors wander off feeling everything is overpriced and inaccessible), and the shops are nothing to write home about, but it definitely has something. Places worth visiting include the impressive Winter Gardens in Church Street built in 1878, the beach and the (free) tower, and the tramway. The latter has been rated top on TripAdvisor and there are now Heritage Tram Tours on trams dating back to the 1990s in single deck Brush Cars et al. You can either hop on or off the trams, or just enjoy a round trip along the route of the illuminations. There are of course the famous evening illumination tours, but check the dates before you go (usually September to November).

Finally, if you wanted to finish with a flavour of what lies beyond, I drove on from Blackpool to Cleveleys and then further to Morecambe Bay. Cleveleys was fascinating in that it illustrates how big a budget a relatively small place can swallow up. In excess of £20 million pounds has been spent already in this little known location as part of a sea defence scheme (all part of a £63 million project to replace 2 kilometres of old sea wall). More plans are muted; if you Google 'Eden Project North' you'll see. It is a while since I studied coasts as part of my geography degree, but one thing I learnt is that if you try to tame the sea in one location, it just shifts the problem alongshore. So the area around and beyond Morecombe could be in for a battering. Do go down to see the bay (before it disappears) and whilst you're there pop into the indoor Fleetwood Market to visit just one great stall 'Oooh Baby' Spanish baby clothes. Special things can be found – alive and kicking – in the most unlikely places.

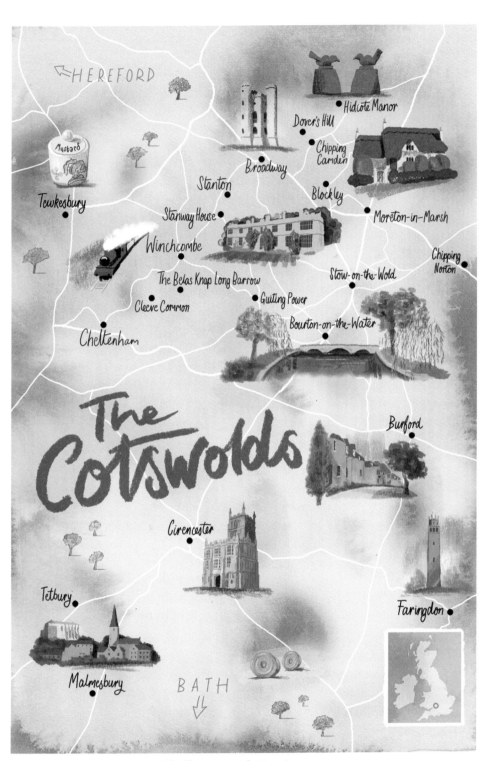

The illustration is by Scott Jessop

The Slaughters near
Bourton-on-the-Water, Cotswolds

Recommended read: *Love in a Cold Climate* by Nancy
Mitford, written when the Mitford sisters lived nearby

A very short mini break that explores the best of the north Cotswolds, staying in a lovely hotel in a quiet spot with great walks on the doorstep. The recommended book was written from Asthall Manor near Burford, which opens its gardens as part of the National Garden Scheme and every other year for a sculpture exhibition. It overlooks the Windrush valley.

Accommodation:

The recommended place to stay – if you feel some luxury is justified – is the Lords of the Manor in the village of Upper Slaughter. It is a privately owned country house hotel with a Michelin star (you can eat out if that is a step too far). It has won lots of awards over the years, and in addition to the comfortable interior, the garden was designed by the Chelsea gold medal winner Julie Toll and includes a wild flower meadow, a walled garden and classic gravel garden. It is worth contacting the hotel directly for the best rates, especially as they often have last minute availability. The website is lordsofthemanor.com and the address Upper Slaughter, Gloucestershire, GL54 2JD. Telephone 01451 820243.

The Slaughters

Upper and Lower Slaughter get their name from 'miry place' relating to the stream on which they are located; the Eye is a tributary to the Windrush. Indeed there is water everywhere. The villages have been much photographed as well as being used as film locations. Upper

Slaughter is a 'sainted village' in that it didn't lose anyone in the First World War – indeed it has a very calm and saintly feel to it. Lower Slaughter is recorded in the Doomsday Book of 1086 as being the site of a mill, which is still there. It was also the retirement destination of RJ Mitchell's son, who wrote a book, *Schooldays to Spitfire*, about the role his father played in designing the single-seater fighter plane made famous for its prominent role in the Battle of Britain. On arrival, the best way to explore the immediate area is to ask the hotel for one of their guided walks. The best one to request is Walk 1, Copse Hill and the Slaughters. It is a 3-mile-long triangular walk that can be shortened by cutting across at the apex. On the route you will see the site of a twelfth century motte and bailey castle, walk on a section of Roman road, admire a dovecot and study a plaque celebrating the wedding of Prince Charles and Diana on the 29th July 1981.

Not far from the hotel is the Jacobean National Trust property Chastleton House (the post code is GL56 0SU, and telephone 01608 674355). It was built between 1607 and 1612 by the wool merchant Walter Jones and remained in the family (who became increasingly impoverished over time) unchanged for over 400 years. It has limited opening hours and is often used for filming, so check before if you go.

The Big Four

No visit to the Cotswolds would be complete without visiting two or more of 'the big four' – Chipping Campden, Broadway, Bourton-on-the-Water and Stow-on-the Wold.

Chipping Campden marks the start of the Cotswold Way. Frequently described as the 'jewel in the crown' of the Cotswold towns, it is also one of the best preserved and most historically important. A planned town of the late twelfth century, the high street followed the line of an important trading route. The ancient word 'Chipping' refers to a market and the market hall, built in 1627, was for the sale of butter, cheese and poultry – remains with its weathered pillars and arches.

Indeed there is an historic atmosphere around many of the buildings like the Market Hall, Grevel House, Woolstaplers Hall and the 'wool church' of St James. Chipping Campden is also known for its Arts and Crafts heritage. In the twentieth century many craftsmen followed William Morris to settle in the area, and the Guild of Handicraft moved from London's East End to what is now the Cotswold House Hotel and Spa (a good stop for coffee). Researching the Cotswolds prior to my visit, I read about the town in JB Priestley's *English Journey* where he wrote, 'There is no Yeo Old Chipping Campden nonsense about it', and almost a century on, this is still the case. It is a working town and it is possible to buy original and inexpensive handmade gifts from rural stores like Sam Wilson's Studio, and wonderful shoes from the independent Molemi, both on or near the high street. For refreshments, you're spoilt for choice, but can't go too far wrong with a pie at the cosy Ebrington Arms (theebringtonarms.co.uk) or Aga baked scones at Badgers Hall (badgershall.com). If time allows, book to visit Hidcote Manor Gardens (details below) whilst you are there.

Broadway next. This is the most 'manicured' of the north Cotswold towns, and depending on the time you get there, can be quite busy – mainly with tourists ogling the many beautiful houses. The town is dominated by a very wide street lined with shops, restaurants and plenty of antique establishments. It is worth a stroll down the main street, stopping to go into the best Oka in the UK (in my opinion) at number 46, and to look at the Scandi Designs in Cotswold Trading at number 36. What you should really be doing, however, is visiting Broadway Tower as can be seen on the illustrated map. It is a Rapunzel-style folly on top of the hill which was built for George William, 6th Earl of Coventry, and designed by Capability Brown (landscape) and James Wyatt (architecture). It was completed in 1798. Members of the Arts and Crafts movement used the tower as a holiday retreat and frequent visitors included William Morris and Dante Gabriel Rossetti. It is open most of the year, and from the top, there are views over sixteen counties (broadwaytower.co.uk).

Bourton-on-the Water is south of the above, and is described as the Venice of the Cotswolds as it straddles the clear water of the Windrush river with six low stone bridges. Frequently voted the prettiest village in England, it is quite an interesting mix of ice cream parlours, tea rooms and cafés, with some odd customs mixed in. Every year for seventy years, for example, there is football in the river, usually on August Bank holiday, and everyone gets a drenching. Woe betide anyone to lark around in the river on a Sunday, however. If you would like to know more, Google 'Old Bill called Cotswold village as row over rubber ducky race gets out of hand'. The town is home to a motor museum and toy collection, see cotswoldmotormuseum.co.uk, which is open daily from mid-February to December. Other attractions include a model village (a replica of Bourton) opened in 1937, Birdland opened twenty years later and a domed tower on St Lawrence church – unique in the Cotswolds.

If you are going for the works, it is Stow-on-the-Wold next. Despite the late AA Gill describing it in his *Angry Island* book of 2005 as 'the worst place in the world'. It has many merits. At 800ft it is the highest Cotswold town and dates from a prehistoric fortified settlement. It had special importance in the English Civil War as it was close by – at Donnington – that the last battle was fought in March 1646. Like most of the Cotswold towns, products for market feature highly, and it was host to some of the largest sheep fairs in the region with 20,000 young animals herded into the square for sale. I suggest you park in the main square opposite Scott's of Stow and with a bag of freshly made vanilla fudge in your hands, walk briskly around the town to get a 'like it or loath it' feel for the place. Then you can say you've been there and done that, and possibly bought the T-shirt.

If you have time visit:

Hidcote Manor Gardens

Open Saturday to Wednesday, Hidcote is one of the country's greatest gardens and is a National Trust property. It is an 'Arts and Crafts inspired' garden that represents the fulfilment of an American's English fantasy. There are intricately designed outdoor 'rooms' full of colour and surprises. The post code is GL55 6LR, telephone 01386 438333. Quoting from the greatbritishgardens.co.uk website, it comprises of a series of small gardens within a garden, but also with long avenues bordered by different plantings. The garden is famous for rare shrubs and trees, as well as its outstanding design features. There are water features, wild flower areas and pools with plenty of places to sit and take in the atmosphere. It recommends you see the long herbaceous borders, which give a great splash of colour from July, and that you walk amongst the old scented roses along the walkway and small garden houses. It is rated as one of the top twenty gardens in the UK.

Harrogate

Yorkshire Dales

North York Moors

Leeds

York

Halifax

Hull

Peak District

Sheffield

Yorkshire

The illustration is by Holly Francesca from West Yorkshire

Halifax in Yorkshire

Recommended read: *A Long Way from Verona* by Jane
Gardam, set in Yorkshire where Gardam has a home

A short break to Halifax isn't on everyone's 'to do' list, but it really
should be. It is both humbling and enlightening. My reason for
choosing it was reading an article in the Times about the renovation of
the Georgian former wool mill, the Piece Hall. It had just had £20
million spent on it and the results are stunning. Described as the north's
best kept secret, it is huge (the courtyard of the building alone is 66,000
square feet), beautiful (grade 1 listed) and virtually unique (the only
surviving cloth hall in the country and one of only three in Europe).
What is good about this trip is that you don't need a car. Fast trains go
direct to Halifax from King's Cross, and once there, everything is within
walking distance or a short train/bus ride away. Included is a visit to
Hebden Bridge. This is the town that was in the news for being badly
flooded in 2015, and has more independent shops than any other town
in the UK.

Accommodation:

The hotel recommended is the Imperial Crown Hotel – just by the
station. The address is 42 Horton Street HX1 1QE (corushotels.com).
It has been chosen for convenience above all else, and the entrance
areas have seen better days, but the bedrooms are fine. This part of
Yorkshire took such a battering with the decline of industry and it is
only now starting to recover, so it seems right therefore to show some
solidarity. If you want to go a bit more upmarket and are prepared to
travel 3 miles outside of Halifax, the best hotel is Holdsworth House
in Holdsworth Road HX2 9TG (holdsworthhouse.co.uk). It featured
in *The Last Tango in Halifax*.

Halifax

Arriving on the train from London and taking an initial stroll around the town, it was like seeing a tale of two cities. Above the eye line was beautiful architecture and wonderful street lights, below, gaudy shop signs for Poundland and the like. Added to this, the town centre seemed to have a demoralised spirit compared to the newly renovated areas. The Piece Hall is in a league of its own. The arrival of the latter has put a spanner in the works of an otherwise downward spiral. This is a town to watch, as people with vision are out to rescue it from degradation, and it is worth it because it is steeped in history. John Betjeman got it right when he described it as 'a town of hidden beauty'.

A brief history:

The best place to visit to understand Halifax's past is the Calderdale Industrial Museum, which is just a stroll along from the hotel entrance in Square Road, HX1 1QG. Check the internet (there is no website but key information is available online) for opening times because it is run by volunteers. From coal and clay mining, to cloth and carpet making and then to machine engineering (and finally sweets), it had been a success story for generations. The town's main fortunes came from the wool textile industry. The production of woollen cloth was seen as the mainstay of the local economy as far back as 1200. In 1276 the world's first guillotine was created specifically for the execution of cloth thieves, who were tried and executed within 24 hours of being caught. The site is signposted in the town but I couldn't find it (you might have better luck). By the sixteenth century the majority of production was still taking place in the home. Every member of the household would be involved in the various processes. However, by the eighteenth century technological advances meant it was more cost effective to manufacture cloth in mills and Halifax became a major industrial town with some of the most extensive factories in the country, renowned especially for carpet production. At its height there were hundreds of individual mills in the town and the largest, Dean Clough, employed 5,000 workers and stretched half-a-mile up the valley. With technological advances and competition from abroad, the twentieth century was a period of relative stagnation and decline. The industrial base was extended with machine tool and parts manufacture, and more recently confectionary (Nestle are located here, and Quality Street is a big export brand), but there are still pockets of depressing wasteland, so visitors are the hope of the future. Banking is still a major employer.

Not to miss when you visit:

The Piece Hall

Built between 1774 and 1779, and paid for by wealthy local merchants (just look at the entrance gates to get an idea of how grand the project was), it was intended to provide a venue for handloom weavers to sell their 30ft lengths of cloth called 'pieces', which they brought in from their home by horse. On a Saturday morning at 10am, two hours of trading took place in 315 rooms. The building is a huge rectangular structure built in a classical style and it is on three levels, all around a wonderful courtyard. The construction of the Piece Hall must have had a dramatic impact not just because of its awesome scale, but also because it created order in a straggling and untidy town.

The Industrial Revolution saw its downfall and the plaza hosted a fish market and was the venue for Halifax's first balloon ascent in 1824. In 1972 the hall was very nearly demolished to make way for a shopping centre. The plans were defeated by a single vote at a council meeting. Renovation wasn't easy, as no detailed plans existed and a graveyard with 217 skeletons was unearthed in the process. It was reopened in the summer of 2017 with a specially composed fanfare involving 150 saxophones. The renovated hall now houses a mixture of bars, unusual shops and cafés, including an ice cream parlour, a retro music store and a fairy shop. The council hopes to attract up to 1.6 million visitors a year and regular arts, music and educational events are planned throughout the year, most of which are free.

No.1 Woolshops, Borough Market, Somerset House and Dean Clough

In the sixteenth century Halifax's streets resembled places like York. Timber-framed, gabled and jettied houses were the norm but more 'red and white' than the conventional 'black and white'. The best (and virtually only) example is now a coffee shop located in the town centre and called No.1 Woolshops. As the years progressed rationalisation of all the different types of markets was necessary and in 1896 the new Borough Market was opened. It is located between Albion and Market Street and is open daily from 9am until 5pm, except on Sundays. It is a grand Victorian cast-iron and glass structure, which is light and airy as well as colourful. Originally it was occupied mainly by butchers, with a separate area for fishmongers. Today it is a mix of stalls not unlike the one in Morecombe, but worth visiting particularly with a tilted head. Not far from Borough Market in Rawson Street is an example of a merchants' house called Somerset House. There were lots of fine houses built in the eighteenth century as a result of the wealth accumulated by leading merchant families. It is difficult to appreciate how big Somerset House was because the east end was demolished in 1897 to make way for what is now Lloyds Bank. It was over 60 metres long, which is the equivalent of three cricket pitches. The main owner was John Royds, a merchant and banker. Finally, stroll down to see Dean Clough Mills. It is well signposted to the north of the town and is an example of how, in the post-industrial economy, new uses can be accommodated within an historic setting. The mills are many stories high and extend over a massive area. Having been originally the carpet weaving works of John Crossley and Sons, they now house offices, industrial units and cultural facilities.

Minster Church of St John the Baptist

The importance of Halifax in the Middle Ages is expressed in this church, located towards the river in the Causeway HX1 1QL (halifaxminster.org.uk). It was built 900 years ago by Benedictine monks, and their tradition still shapes the worship, education and hospitality there today. Start by studying the outside, focusing on the gargoyles on the south side, then see the graves of clothiers in the mid-1800s. Inside is interesting too, particularly the window of Nathaniel. Dorothy Waterhouse donated these 'Commonwealth windows' in 1652 in the chancel. They have clear glazing in small panes, arranged to give a pattern of stars and diamonds. The simplicity of the glazing reflects the puritanical thinking of the era, which saw the triumph of Cromwell's Roundheads over royalist exuberance.

Recommended places to eat in Halifax include Ricci's Kitchen, 01422 740001, which is towards the north end of the town, and the new performing arts centre in Square Chapel (squarechanel.co.uk). This is an amazing addition to the Piece Hall, with great food too. I enjoyed a delicious fish pie – followed by a fascinating one-man production of *Team Viking* by James Rowland. Described in the blurb as 'Joyous'. It was.

Also visit:

Hebden Bridge

A 'must' on your visit is to take the short train ride to the lovely small town of Hebden Bridge. It is known for having more independent shops than anywhere else in the UK, and as the resting place for Sylvia Plath. Regarding the latter, she is actually buried in the adjoining hilltop village of Heptonstall, near the parents of her husband Ted Hughes. The best way to explore is to head straight for the tourist information centre on the main road (just past the old cinema) and pick up a map and the blue town centre trail booklet. This booklet is the key, because it is easy to miss the best bits without it, plus there are photographs showing 'before' and 'after'. Highlights for me were the Packhorse Bridge, the wonderful shops on Market Street (one of which supplies Harrods with soap, and another, the Heart Gallery, has collections of work by up-and-coming designer makers), and strolling down beyond the Little Theatre (number 9 in the booklet) to walk along the canal towpath. You will be spoilt for choice where to have your lunch. Shibden Hall I didn't have time to visit, but it is easy to get there by bus. They run every 7 minutes from stand B in the bus station, and it is just three or four stops. It is a timber-framed 'house' with an open hall in the centre and cross-wings. It was built by the Otes family in the late fifteenth century and illustrates the increasing prosperity of Halifax at the time. Anne Lister, the diarist, lived there in the early nineteenth century. She employed the landscape designer Mr Gray of York to create a park with terraces, woodland plantations, a lake and a Gothic entrance and lodge. The website is museums.calderdale.gov.uk Lister's Road HX3 6XG. It is open daily except on a Friday.

The illustration is a limited edition print by Chris Snow of Maps and Diagrams

Tenby in South Wales

Recommended read: *My Year* by Roald Dahl; Dahl enjoyed
seaside holidays here in the 1920s and 1930s
It is quite difficult to find, so alternatively
The Hourglass by Tracy Rees

If you choose a good time of year (and avoid Sunday and Monday), Tenby is a great mini break. Like Swanage, it is a slightly faded old Victorian seaside town with none of the usual shops, cafés and restaurants that can be seen elsewhere. It has narrow cobbled streets, colourful architecture and varied sea views all around. I was inspired to visit by reading Bill Bryson's description in *The Road to Little Dibbling*, 'I had heard that it was a charming place, but in fact it is exquisite – full of pastel-coloured houses, sweet-looking hotels and guest-houses, characterful pubs and cafes, glorious beaches and gorgeous views.' It also featured in Grand Designs for the conversion of the RNLI Lifeboat Station for residential use in 2011. The architect was W. T. Douglas and it is available to view online.

Getting there:

Depending on where you are travelling from, I recommend that you take the Severn Bridge and aim for the M49 rather than following the M4 the whole way. I stopped at Clifton in Bristol to break the journey, and had coffee in the Ivy just off the square before driving across Clifton Bridge. Highly recommended, especially as there are a couple of lovely dress shops just opposite.

Accommodation:

Because golf widows aren't (always) self-indulgent, I chose the Panorama Hotel overlooking the south beach on the Esplanade, SA70 7DU, telephone 01834 844976. The owner, Debbie, insisted on an upgrade to a sea view room. Indeed, all the people I met in Tenby were kind and helpful. The website is panoramahotel.co.uk and the breakfasts are lovely.

A brief history of the walled town:

Tenby's roots date back to the time of the Norman Conquest when the country was invaded and colonised around 1093. The medieval castle walls were built by the Pembrokeshire Earls in 1264 to fortify the town from Welsh rebellion, and have remained remarkably intact to the present day. The pretty harbour was a thriving port in the Middle Ages, with cargoes arriving from Spain, Portugal and France. Merchants became rich on products like salt, and built fine houses inside the walled town. The church of St Mary's reflects the town's prosperity at this time.

The town was popularised by Sir William Paxton after the Victorians began visiting the town for its health benefits. It was a Mecca for the well-to-do holiday maker of the day. A memorial to Queen Victoria's consort, Prince Albert, was inaugurated in 1865 and is to be found a short distance from the Victorian bandstand on the seafront near castle hill. The Industrial Revolution arrived in the form of railway lines and shipping lanes and the tourist industry boomed.

The artist Augustus John was born in Tenby and (apparently) spent a miserable childhood in a house on Victoria Street. His mother died of rheumatic gout when he was six years old and his father was a cold replacement. It is said that he showed no artistic talent until he fell whilst diving off rocks in the bay and emerged a 'genius'. John Sargent later described him as the best draughtsman since the Renaissance.

Not to miss when you visit:

The National Trust's Tudor Merchants House

To understand Tenby's early wealth it is worth making this your first visit. Built in the fifteenth century, and still furnished and decorated in authentic Tudor fixtures and fittings, it illustrates the lifestyle of a successful merchant, and the time. His table is set with pewter and glass, positioned on a smart woven mat and placed at a higher level to that of the servants. When I visited, there were guides in each of the rooms who explained all the pertinent facts. The house has limited opening hours and might need to be pre-booked so check before you go on 0344249 1895 (tudormerchantshouse@nationaltrust.org.uk). It is located down a narrow alleyway in the centre of town called Quay Hill.

A great place for coffee or lunch afterwards is the Qube which is just around the corner on the main street, and opposite is the lovely Baytree restaurant run by the hugely efficient owner Karen.

Tenby Museum and Art Gallery

The oldest independent museum in Wales, established in 1878, but closed on a Sunday and Monday (contrary to what it might say on the website tenbymuseum.org.uk). In the gallery you can learn about Henry Tudor's legendary escape from the town, discover which Tenby-born mathematician invented the equals (=) sign and discover Tenby's involvement in the D-Day landings. Look out for the nineteenth century Milton Monk's Rock meat plate, and John Speed's map of Pembrokeshire from the seventeenth century.

Having visited the museum walk behind the building up onto castle hill to admire the views. On a clear day you can see Monkstone Point, Worms Head and the coast of Devon. There is an information board attached to the castle ruins that points out places of interest, and this is also where Prince Albert's statue can be found. Look down towards the water and both the new and old lifeboat centres can be seen. Both were closed to visitors when I was there, but it is worth wandering down to take a look.

Caldey Island

There are many boat trips from Tenby harbour, but the one recommended is to the monastic island of Caldey. It is open to visitors from Easter to October, although not on a Sunday or in bad weather (telephone 01834 844453). Further details can be found on caldeyislandwales.com

The island has been inhabited since the Stone Age and has been home to various orders of monks from Celtic times. The present inhabitants are monks of the Cistercian Order and they live in an imposing white building with a red turreted roof. Look out for the Abbey Church. This is where the monks begin their seven daily services at 3.30am. Pleasingly the island isn't commercialised and the shop offers products produced on the island, from shortbread made in the monastery to perfume made on the island since the 1950s. An information sheet is available when you book, which directs you to other points of interest on the island, including the island post office and a museum.

The Old Town Hall and Market

Located in the central shopping area off the high street, this is a listed building. TripAdvisor will say there isn't much to see – which is true, unless you look more carefully, particularly at the rear façade off Upper Frog Street. It was originally built of stone on the ground floor in 1829, then an upper storey of stucco was added in 1860. Internally there are iron balustrades, an old framed document with the 'tolls' for selling meat and fish, and a wall montage depicting Tenby's history. This last is 32ft by 8ft and was painted by local artist Eric Bradforth.

The Walled Garden at Upton Castle

Upton Castle is a picturesque Norman Castle which remains a private family home. The garden consists of 35 acres surrounded by ancient woodland. There are herbaceous borders, a formal rose garden and a traditional nineteenth century walled garden. The address is Cosheston, SA72 4SE. Telephone 01646 689996. Opening times vary, so check before you go. The reviews are mixed so miss it if time is tight!

Try not to miss on your way home:

Dylan Thomas's Boathouse at Laugharne

This is amazing - so do try to go even if it means missing other things on the trip. There are two things to see, the writing shed, which is exactly as he left it and where he wrote many of his finest works, and the boathouse where Dylan Thomas lived with his wife Caitlin and their children Lleweln, Aeronwy and Colm. Dylan said there was nowhere else like the boathouse, and indeed you can see the world as he knew it, as nothing has changed - the views are lovely and everything is unbelievably peaceful. A very special place.

The entrance is reached along a cliff path, and once there, a short film explains his life and works (he died of alcohol poisoning aged 39 in America). It is on three floors with a café in the basement. Hot cheese scones are my recommendation.

It is run by Carmarthenshire County Council and open from 11am Thursday to Monday. Pre-booking isn't required but only 12 visitors are allowed in at any one time so arrive early (dylanthomasboathouse.com). The address is Dylan's Walk, Laugharne, SA33 4SD.

The illustration is by Sarah Farooqi from Northumberland

Alnwick in Northumberland

Recommended read: *In Too Deep* by Bea Davenport, a debut novel inspired by a medieval fair held in Alnwick

Many friends had said 'You must go to Alnwick – you would love it', so I succumbed, and yes I did. More than two nights are recommended to do it justice. To some extent, it sums up what is special about this country.

Accommodation:

The very best place to stay – in all respects – is the Cookie Jar. It isn't cheap, but worth every penny. It is beautifully decorated, and surprisingly doesn't tell you much about itself until you arrive. What it plays down is that it is a former convent housed in an historic building. There are eleven luxurious rooms, including one in the former chapel which spans the width of the building and has stunning stained-glass windows. I stayed in Linehope Spout, named after the waterfall, and it overlooked Alnwick Castle. Luxury was everywhere, from the Hypnos bed, to the Penhaligon toiletries, to the lovely roll-top bath. If this trip comes after the Hereford monastery, it will be quite a leap. Suffice to say the key person behind the desk (Brindley) was previously the valet of the 11th Duke of Northumberland (he was unfortunately the person who also found him dead). The address is Bailiffgate, Alnwick, NE66 1LU. Telephone 01665 510465 (cookiejaralnwick.com).

Alnwick

Alnwick was voted best town in the UK in Country Life about the time the Harry Potter film came out and Alnwick Gardens opened, and again in the Times in 2018. It is an historic market town and has become one of the country's top tourist destinations – without getting too touristy. It is just 5 miles from Northumberland's heritage coastline and roughly in the centre of the County, equidistant from Berwick and Newcastle – hence a great base from which to explore, plus it is easy to get to, being just off the A1. The town isn't big, dates back to AD 600, and is full of old buildings and cobbled streets all positioned around a lovely market square.

A brief history:

Edward V1 made Alnwick the county town of Northumberland, but its history is very much linked to the numerous bloody battles between the Percy family (the Duke of Northumberland's Percy ancestors took possession of the castle in 1309) and the Scots. On a hill facing the castle on the north bank of the Aln sits a large stone cross, which commemorates the killing of King Malcolm III of Scotland whilst invading on the outskirts of the town. Indeed there are emblems of the past all around the town that are comprehensively explained on the town trail. What isn't really mentioned is that inside the White Swan Hotel, the lounge has fittings from the *RMS Olympic,* which was identical to the *RMS Titanic* and the *RMS Gigantic.* Both were destroyed after the sinking of the Titanic in 1912 because of fears that they would meet the same fate. It is worth a drink inside (but probably not a meal). The best starting point to this trip therefore, is to pick up the flier for the Alnwick Town Trail from the tourist information office in the market square and explore the immediate environs on foot. There are four zones on the map (the Castle Quarter, Market District, Bondgate Within and Bondgate Without) with forty-three stops – which although it is less than 2 miles in total, is realistically too much, so ideally just focus on the lower numbers nearer the centre. There is also an open top bus ride around the town that can be accessed from the large car park behind the square, but it only runs on limited days/times, so check first.

Not to miss when you visit:

Alnwick Castle

The castle began as a simple Norman motte and bailey and was replaced in the twelfth century by a stone fortress. It fell into decay after the border wars, and was restored in the eighteenth century by Robert Adam. During the nineteenth century, the 4th Duke of Northumberland transformed the castle into a great country house. The interior is decorated in a fine Italian Renaissance style and contains paintings by Canaletto, Tintoretto, Van Dyke and Titian. This is what makes it such an amazing place to visit – on the outside it is a classical castle, like so many other castles in the country, but inside it could be the grandest of country houses. The castle ranks as one of the most magnificent medieval fortresses in the country. The gateway is guarded by an impressive barbican, and the outline of its massive keep, walls and towers completely dominate the town's horizon. Parts of the castle are open to the public, including the Constable's Tower, the Postern Tower, the keep and many of its exquisitely furnished state rooms. The visit is all the more interesting because the 12th Duke of Northumberland and his family live there for part of the year and the interior reflects this with family photographs, stuffed animals (the Duchess is a fan of taxidermy), and an amazing drinks cabinet. In recent years the castle has taken a star role in numerous film and television productions – most noteworthy Hogwarts School of Witchcraft and Wizardry, and Downton Abbey. It is open April to October daily from 10am–6pm (alnwickcastle.com).

Alnwick Garden

The Duchess of Northumberland's garden at Alnwick is described as a 'contemporary pleasure garden and community asset' but it is much more than that. At a cost of £50 million, it is said to be 'The Versailles of the North', but it is also a registered charity. It contributes to the local economy, helps disabled and unemployed people to have worthwhile work and has put the whole area on the map.

After a long battle with English Heritage, who said that she was responsible for the destruction of one of the greatest gardens in the country, it attracted 330,000 visitors in its first year. It certainly isn't conventional, but neither is she: Jane Percy is a commoner who met her future husband when he was at Eton, she followed him to Oxford where he read history and she took a secretarial course. They married in 1979, had four children and then were thrown into taking on Alnwick Castle when Ralph Percy's brother unexpectedly died. She has done many extraordinary things beyond establishing the garden, including cage fighting! Like it or not, she has achieved something amazing, and full credit to her for having the confidence and courage to carry it off.

Each section of the garden has more to it than meets the eye. William Pye's water sculptures, for example, are used by school science groups to explore laws of gravity and water surface tension. The hornbeam-covered walkway occasionally houses groups of Tai Chi practitioners, the Poison Garden is used to pass on drug and drink awareness and the polytunnels shelter groups of children, making bug hotels and herb baskets. It is also a wedding venue. There is a café, but I highly recommend that you book to go back in the evening and eat in the unusual treetop restaurant, which is lit with fairy lights and serves lovely food. Telephone 01665 511852. Just spray your legs with insect repellent before you go.

Alnwick Gardens is open from February to October daily from 10am, see alnwickgardens.com.

Barter Books

This is one of Europe's biggest second-hand bookshops and it is to be found in an old railway station. To explain why this is such a wonderful place to visit I am going to quote extracts from the business section of a Journal which was written in June 2013 that basically tells their story:

> *The owners, Mary and Stuart Manley, met when he threw her a note during a transatlantic plane journey ... Mary was returning to the UK after visiting her father in Missouri, and Englishman Stuart was on his way home. 'I opened it up and it said: "if you want to talk to me, raise your hand",' says Mary. 'I'd asked for a*

seat on my own because I just wanted to read a book, I didn't want to hear some man talking about how his wife didn't understand him. But this was too good – so I raised my hand, Stuart sat down, and basically in the course of the flight, he told me how his wife didn't understand him (laughs). He was getting divorced, and I thought, "this isn't good". But it ended up really well; we got married three years later.' Stuart puts it down to acting on his luck.

Luck is something the pair admit they've been blessed with since opening Barter Books in Alnwick's former railway station in 1991. At the time, Stuart was making models for rail modellers and war gamers, in part of the building. 'I ran it for ten years and it was singularly unsuccessful. We had just done a remarketing with new packaging and we'd hocked our all into the bank and it doubled sales, but we needed to triple sales to get us out of trouble. In those days of twenty years back, interest rates were so high, we were just heading for the rocks. We were paying back the interest, but we weren't paying back the loan. We were heading for bankruptcy at high speed – then Mary had her little idea.'

Mary worked in an antiquarian bookshop in the US and taught art history before coming to the UK to study at St John's College in Oxford. 'As I tell people often, there's nothing more inspiring than an overdraft. The only thing I knew anything about was books; it was either teaching or working in a bookshop. In 1991, I needed something to do, needed money and I'd always wanted a bookshop – but only second hand. I was driving up to Lindisfarne, because I was doing voluntary work, and I thought maybe I could start a second-hand bookshop and call it Barter Books, have a little barter system. Stuart liked the idea and said "let's give it a go". Starting off in a tiny part of the building, which was built in the 1880s and closed as a station in 1968, Barter Books grew and grew.'

They would make a bit of money but then throw it back into the shop. A labour of love that now pays off. Among the 350,000 books are 'hundreds' of antiquarian books priced £1,000-plus including *a £17,000, 17th Century Italian volume on inventions. There are about forty employees, a mixture of full and part-time ranging from café staff to book valuers and web experts.*

Barter Books, however, is as much of an experience as a shop, which is a combination of Mary's vision and Stuart's business nous. From the very beginning, Mary gave the then tiny shop a distinctive look with giant round lampshades. As the business expanded into other parts of the Victorian building, she discovered and restored the original fixtures and fittings including a number of marble-topped fireplaces in what were the waiting rooms, the hatch where tickets were issued, and a drinking fountain with metal cups. She is justifiably proud of the giant author mural she commissioned from local artist Peter Dodd, which features forty-three famous writers and characters ranging from Jane Austen to Tom Stoppard. The stunning picture took two years to complete. Dodd's work is featured elsewhere in the building including a portrait of Alnwick's last 'top hat' station master John Patterson, in what was the first class ladies' waiting room. Today, the Manleys live in what was the stationmaster's house.

The business is now as much a tourist attraction as a bookshop. The couple have produced a walkabout booklet that customers can pick up to explore the building. Model trains run on tracks on top of the book columns near the front of the shop; they have now travelled around 30,000 miles. Professional speakers appear once a month. A final word from Stuart: 'All my weaknesses are countered by her strengths, but also very much vice-versa. If ever there was a true partnership, this is it … even down to the M&S bit!'

Barter Books address is Alnwick Station, Wagon Way Road, NE66 2NP (barterbooks.co.uk). Check for opening times.

Craigside

Described as 'the home of hydroelectricity', this is a mock Tudor mansion near Rothbury built by Norman Shaw and now owned by the National Trust. It was built in 1863 as a simple country getaway for industrialist and inventor William Armstrong, later to become the 1st Baron Armstrong. An engineer, scientist and philanthropist, Armstrong is remembered as the father of modern artillery. In 1880 Baron Armstrong called upon architect Richard Norman Shaw to transform his house into a state of the art mansion, an elaborate country house in Tudor style, incorporating a science laboratory and an astronomical observatory. The Armstrongs were avid collectors, and the house is filled with British art, furniture and ceramics, as well as scientific curiosities, and exhibits of natural history. One of the highlights is a sculpture by John Bell of a slave girl.

David Ross of Britain Express Heritage explains:

'In its day, Cragside was a house of wonders, with features that we take for granted today, but were the very cutting edge of technology and innovation in the late Victorian period. Lord Armstrong introduced extraordinary gadgets and features like a passenger lift, fire alarm buttons throughout the house, a Turkish bath suite, and a peculiar new invention called a telephone. He was more than an inventor; he was also a landscape gardener. He laid out five lakes on the Cragside estate, and planted over 7,000,000 trees and shrubs. One of the unexpected side benefits of all those trees is that the endangered British red squirrel has settled in the Cragside woodland.'

What the house is most well known for, however, is that it was the first building in the world to be lit by hydroelectric power. In 1868 an hydraulic engine was installed, using water to power electrical appliances like a lift, a rotisserie and a clothes washer. How it all works can be seen near the house. It is a sad fact that the Armstrongs had no children, so much of the estate was left to nieces and nephews, who didn't manage things very well. Many of the artwork was sold to pay debts and they weren't necessarily related to death duties (if you get my drift). It is worth asking the National Trust guides about what happened after their death.

Final note: the best way to see the grounds of Cragside is to hop on the little 'bus' that can be found near the rear of the house on the carriage drive. The house is open 10am–5pm, but not necessarily throughout the year, so check nationaltrust.org.uk before you go.

Howick Hall and the Earl Grey Tea Room

Not very well publicised, but definitely worth a visit if you like gardens and tea, are the gardens at Howick Hall to the north-east of Alnwick (howickhallgardens.com) located at NE66 3LB. The estate has been in the Grey family since 1319 and is in the process of being developed into a botanical haven. There are guided tours on Monday and Friday at 2pm between April and October. Telephone 01665 577191 if interested, but going it alone is good too, and the garden is open most of the year except from mid-November to early February. Tea is served in a grand dining room and the story of how the family missed out on securing the rights to Earl Grey Tea (although they invented it) is explained on the menu.

Craster and lunch at the Ship Inn at Low Newton

Crab is a speciality in the area and the recommendation (generally) is to visit the Jolly Fisherman pub in Caster for lunch. It is definitely worth going to Caster to look around, but for the very best crab experience head for the Ship Inn at Low Newton by the sea. Get there early, however, because even the locals are prepared to queue. Next door is a micro-brewery, and within the enclave is a lovely green and a wonderful beach. The post code is NE66 3EL.

Depending on how much time you have (and watch the tide!):

Holy Island

If you can, travel across the causeway to Holy Island and discover a magical place. Home of Lindisfarne Castle and owned by the National Trust. It was converted by Sir Edwin Lutyens into a private holiday home for Edward Hudson, the founder of Country Life. It reopened recently after 100 years of damage from wind and rain. There are regular art exhibitions, lime kilns to explore, and a small Jekyll garden. From the headland at Castle Point, there are views of the Farne Islands where puffins are in abundance. The crossing is dependent on the tides, so some research is necessary before you set off. The postcode is TD15 2SH (lindisfarne@nationaltrust.org.uk).

Tewkesbury visitor information illustrated map

Tewkesbury in Gloucestershire

Recommended read: *Perfect* by Rachel Joyce, the
award-winning Gloucestershire author

Another dip into the Cotswolds, staying in a tiny one bedroom house
– new to the market.

Accommodation:

Sometimes it is nice to be independent – and not have to get
dressed for breakfast – so it was good to find that 'Gina and Jen'
had an immaculate town centre cottage available for two nights to
rent (with free parking). I was fortunate in that everything was
brand new and found it via booking.com. The address is 3
Cotswold cottages, Tewkesbury, GL20 5GH. It is tucked away down
an alley and very quiet, yet close to everything. It was extremely
good value. There is no website so Google booking.com with the
address above and it comes up under Town Centre Cottage. It also
appears on gites.fr. I got the feeling they lived next door, but I could
be wrong.

Tewskesbury

The town lies where the Severn and Avon rivers meet and it offers
one of the best medieval townscapes in England. Timber-framed,
mellow brick houses and narrow alleyways surround the twelfth
century Benedictine Abbey. The Heritage Centre is in the Old Hat
Shop. Tewkesbury was known to Shakespeare (Falstaff has the line
'his wit's as thick as Tewkesbury Mustard') and Dickens (who had
in mind the Royal Hope Pole Inn when writing *Pickwick Papers*).
Tewkesbury mustard can be bought from the local deli. A good
time to visit is July – partly because you're unlikely to see your
golfing spouse during that month – and partly because they host a

festival that re-enacts the Battle of Tewkesbury, the decisive War of the Roses in 1471. The battle map is from a leaflet that can be viewed online from visittewkesbury.info under Battle Walk. The suggestion is that you start by following the walk (which is explained on page 83).

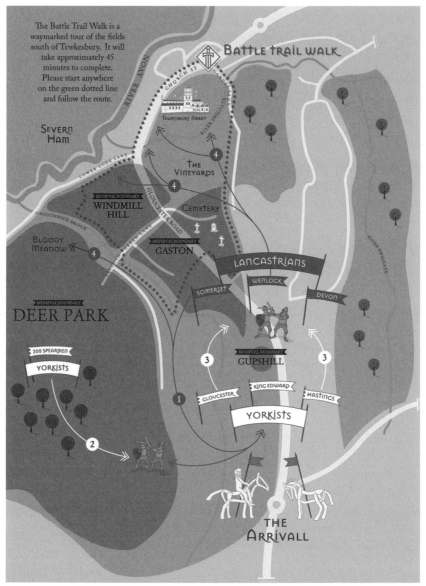

Battle trail walk courtesy of Tewkesbury Borough Council

In summary, the War of the Roses wasn't about principles and firmly-held beliefs, it was about power. Both sides were Plantagenets, tracing their lines back to King Edward 111. This final battle opened with the Lancastrian army (red) forming lines with the Yorkists (white) marching to meet them. The Lancastrians came off worst despite the Duke of Somerset attempting a diversionary movement by attacking from behind (1 on the map). It resulted in his men being attacked by 200 mounted knights who were hiding in the woodland of the deer park (2). The Lancastrian army (not involved in the diversion), were said to stand and watch in horror. Retreat followed as the Yorkists advanced (3) and escape towards the abbey (4), which resulted in further devastation. It is thought that around 2,000 Lancastrians were killed, including Edward, the Price of Wales.

There are other walking routes around the town, and a 45-minute boat ride along the river – which I would highly recommend (pick up a fabulous ice cream sundae from the Ice Cream Cottage in St Mary's Lane before you go, to cheer yourself up after the Battle Walk). The boat is a twelve-seater that operates on a 'first come first served' basis starting at 12 noon every day in July and August, but only on a Wednesday to Sunday in June, September and October. The mooring is located 'Back of Avon', i.e. behind the Avon car park, Waterside, Tewkesbury GL20 5AQ (severnleisurecruises.co.uk).

I used the town mainly as a base to visit nearby – eating out each evening at a great café near the cross roundabout in Church Street called Rosado Lounge (thelounges.co.uk). It is a brightly coloured and spacious café with friendly staff (albeit rather over obsessed with allergies), and numerous portraits on the walls. I was tempted by the pricier Abbot's Table in Church Street but it was full of dating couples so (unusually) I felt a bit uncomfortable, but would go another time, theabbotstable.co.uk. Otherwise there wasn't a wide choice, and in hindsight a meal at Gina and Jen's would have been sensible.

Gloucester

The country town is worth a visit because it has a wealth of ancient buildings and monuments that have been witness to numerous defining moments in British history. The city centre was looking rather run down when I visited, but the key is to see above and beyond, and then you will find beautiful buildings on almost every corner. Whilst there, spend as much money as you can to help the town pull itself up to the level it deserves. Having said that, I notice public and private sectors have recently come together to launch an ambitious £20 million City Centre Regeneration bid – so watch this space.

These are some highlights:

The eleventh-century Gloucester Cathedral, resting place of King Edward II, the last time an English monarch was crowned outside of Westminster Abbey (the nine-year old Henry III in 1216). It is also the home of the majestic Great East Window, which is the size of a tennis court and was installed in the 1350s possibly to commemorate the Battle of Crecy in 1343 and depicts medieval society hierarchically. Interestingly, during World War II, the glass was removed and stored in the crypt, however, the labels got slightly mixed up, so that after the war restorers had to piece the window together using old black and white postcards to work out the final placement. More recently the cathedral has been used as a film and television location to shoot scenes for *Harry Potter* as well as *Wolf Hall* and *Doctor Who*.

The historic Gloucester Docks (just a short walk away) is the next destination, with its lovely waterfront, converted warehouses and an array of restaurants and bars. This area has already been through the process of regeneration (Google 'what Gloucester quays looked like before, during and after construction in gloucestershirelive'). I just dipped a toe in, but research shows that a ship canal was opened here in 1827, allowing boats to bypass sections of the River Severn, making Gloucester an inland port. At its busiest it would have been full of narrow boats, sailing ships and steam barges. Alongside the water were great engineering firms like Fielding and Platt, who manufactured hydraulic machinery for export all over the world. The area has been used to shoot scenes for *Alice Through the Looking Glass* and *Amazing Grace*.

The Tailor of Gloucester Beatrix Potter Museum, which is located in the original building used by Beatrice Potter in her story *The Tailor of Gloucester* (a real-life mystery based on the city's tailor John Pritchard). This museum has excellent reviews on Google so is to be commended. It can be found at 9 College Court, GL1 2NJ (tailor-of-gloucester.org.uk).

Cheltenham

I know Cheltenham quite well, and when visiting tend to get there early for breakfast on the promenade, which is the part of the town with the best shops and cafés. As the UK's most complete Regency town, it is worth completing a brief 'tour'. Start in Montpellier at the end of the promenade south of the town centre. This area was originally developed in the 1830s in conjunction with the spas, then take a walk down the promenade (home to Cavendish House which is Cheltenham's oldest department store), and up to Pittville Park to the north of Cheltenham. The latter was opened in 1825 and is a large ornamental park with Pump Room and lakes. There is lots to do and see in Cheltenham, so depending on your interests (and the day you are there), I would suggest heading over to the Holst Victorian House (open Tuesday to Saturday 10am–4pm) which was the birthplace of the composer Gustav Holst. The house is a time capsule of nineteenth century life with a working kitchen, Victorian bedroom, scullery and nursery. Visitors can also experience a Regency sitting room with an impressive art collection. It can be found at 4 Clarence Road, Cheltenham, GL52 2AY, telephone 01242 524845 (holstvictorianhouse.org.uk).

Alternatively, if you can justify the time, visit the outskirts of Cheltenham (at Coxhorne Farm London Road GL52 6UY) and enjoy of tour of Sibling Gin Distillery. A two-hour visit will give you a tour around the distillery and a tasting of their gin. Book in advance on 07882 125969 siblingdistillery.com, or just pop in to stock up as I did.

Cirencester

This was on my route home (as was Marlborough, which is worth a visit together with Hungerford – if you have the energy).

As the capital of the Cotswolds, Cirencester is a lovely market town. In Roman times 'Corinium Dobunnorum' was the second largest town to London. During the sixth century fortunes changed and the Saxons destroyed it, renaming the place 'Coryn Ceasre'. It became a very prosperous wool town in the medieval period, which is the basis for its charm with honey-coloured stone buildings in narrow streets that you see today.

Cirencester's market town status is mentioned in the Doomsday Book of 1086 and there are still regular markets today. The market place is the heart of the town and is home to a Charter Market (every Monday and Friday) and a Farmers' Market (every 2nd and 4th Saturday of the month). Cirencester's Corn Hall also boasts a regular programme of markets, which include a Home Fashion and Garden Bazaar (from Monday to Thursday), an Antiques and Collectables Market (on Fridays) and the Original Craftsman's Market (1st and 3rd Saturdays). I bought a colour changing umbrella when I was there.

In addition, there are a variety of quality independent shops and cafés so these, together with a dip into the very grand St John Baptist church and the Abbey Grounds behind, add up to a couple of pleasurable hours.

The two places recommended in the guide books (I didn't have time to go) are the Corinium Museum, which is home to one of the largest collections of Romano-British antiquities in the UK. Here you can experience life as a Roman and marvel at the stunning mosaics. It is in Park Street GL7 2BX, 01285 655611 (coriniummuseum.org), and the Roman Amphitheatre. This last is a short walk from the town centre, and is an English Heritage site. Now grassed over, it was built in the early second century as part of a grand scheme of Roman town planning, and had a capacity of 8,000 spectators. Amazing.

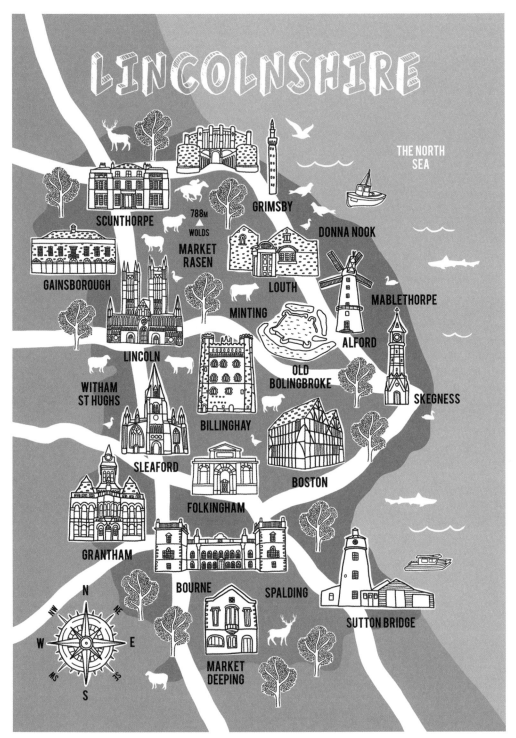

The illustration is by Bea Baranowska

Lincoln in Lincolnshire

Recommended read: *The Mill on the Floss* by George Eliot; it
is based around an imaginary village researched when Eliot
(real name Mary Ann Evans) visited Gainsborough in
Lincolnshire in 1859 with her partner George Lewis

This is the ideal destination for a short city break, especially if you
plan to stay as fit as your golfing partner, because Lincoln has an
'uphill' and 'downhill' joined by the aptly named Steep Hill, voted
Britain's Best Street.

Accommodation:

I stayed in a luxury B&B in glorious countryside just outside Lincoln
in Grange de Lings. It is called Bridleways (bridlewaybandb.co.uk),
post code LN2 2LY. It is run by an artist who can be contacted on
01522 545693. Most of the accommodation is housed in a separate
block – so it felt less personal than staying in the owner's house. The
décor was pretty, and the breakfasts really good.

A brief history of Lincoln:

Lincoln's history can be traced back to 300 BC with a settlement
around Brayford Waterfront by the name of Lindon: 'Lindo'
translating as 'Pool'. Indeed, the Witham Shield, which belonged to a
local tribal chief, was found here and is housed in the British
Museum. Romans, Vikings, Saxons, Normans and other civilisations
made Lincoln their home, and there is evidence everywhere, from
third century Roman stone to Viking place names such as Bailgate,
Danesgate, Wragby and Skellingthorpe, and in 1068 William the
Conqueror led the Norman invasion to the city and ordered the
building of Lincoln Castle, and later Lincoln Cathedral. This last
became the tallest building in the world in 1300 and held the title

until 1549 when the spire collapsed during a storm. When King John placed his seal on the Magna Carta at Runnymede in 1215, a copy was brought back to Lincoln by the Bishop of Lincoln, Hugh of Wells, with the address 'LINCOLNIA' written on the back.

In more recent times, Lincoln was supported by the wool trade, then during the Industrial Revolution engineering was key, particularly through the production of air engines and tanks. Indeed, in 1916 the first ever tanks were designed and built in Lincoln, giving the city the nickname 'Tank Town'. These machines were paraded through the city before going to war with – soon after – one in fourteen wartime aircraft being produced here. It is still a world leader in the engineering industry.

Lincoln

I started my tour at the tourist information office in an attractive Tudor building in Castle Square, at the top of Steep Hill. From here you can pick up a map to guide you around the city. The best place to start is Lincoln Castle, which is nearing the end of a £22 million restoration project. Inside there is a Victorian prison (closed when I was there), designed to separate prisoners that could otherwise corrupt. Men, women and children as young as eight were held there from 1848 to 1878 for a range of crimes, from petty theft to highway robbery and murder. John Nicholson, the prison governor, in 1854 wrote on the 15th of April 'William Messenger placed in dark cell on bread and water for 3 days for destroying prison books and insolence'. There is also a working courthouse designed by Robert Smirke, who was the British Museum architect.

From the castle a stroll around Bailgate, which is just around the corner. It is lined with independent cafés, shops and quirky alleyways. Look out for various plaques on the walls as the history of the various sections is well documented. Fortified by a coffee (and maybe plum bread from a bakery such as Curtis), tackle Steep Hill. It is just beyond Exchequer Gate and is narrow, cobbled and seriously inclined. Look as you go at the Georgian houses mixed with half-timber Tudor properties and see the Trent valley in the distance.

The little shops are interesting too, until you reach the flat bottom (and beyond), when everything suddenly changes from very special to very ordinary. Most cities have a mix, so get back up to the top as soon as possible and pop into the cathedral.

A decent stroll from the cathedral at Burton Road, postcode LN1 3LY is the Museum of Lincolnshire Life (lincolnshire.gov.uk). It is housed in a Victorian barracks built for the Royal North Militia in 1857. It is an eclectic mix, but successfully reflects the social history from about 1700 to the present day. It has a little café which employs staff with some learning difficulties, which is really nice.

One other place to see in Lincoln is the Usher Gallery. Opened in 1927, following a bequest to the city from the jeweller James Ward Usher, it houses some amazing art and decorative pieces. Here you can see views of Lincoln by artists such as LS Lowry and JMW Turner, admire contemporary vases by Grayson Perry and enjoy Usher's collection of English and French watches.

Doddington Hall and Gardens

Begun in 1595 by Robert Smythson, one of England's foremost Elizabethan architects, Doddington Hall was completed in 1600 and has never been sold since. It is a lived-in family home with a 400-year history of unbroken family occupation, which has resulted in an amazing collection of furniture, paintings, ceramics and household objects throughout. It also highlights the challenges of looking after such an estate in the twenty-first century. The present custodians are Claire and James Birch, who are continuing the work of her parents by developing the various areas of the estate from the fabulous farm shop, to the home and clothes stores, the wedding and events business, as well as increasing access to the public, albeit mainly through estate walks (for which it is possible to download a leaflet from the doddingtonhall.com site under estate walks). The hall itself is open on selected dates, mainly Wednesdays, Fridays, Sundays and bank holidays from April 6th. Tickets need to be booked in advance but if you visit outside of these days, there is a virtual tour on the website – which takes some getting used to, but does give a flavour of how amazing it all is. The address is Main Street, Doddington, Lincoln, LN6 4RU and the website is doddingtonhall.com. There is plenty of parking over the road and it is definitely worth visiting for the café and shop/s alone, as the rest is a bonus.

Grantham and Woolsthorpe Manor

One of the best parts of my trip was learning about Newton by visiting the National Trust property Woolsthorpe Manor near Grantham. You need to book (nationaltrust.org.uk), as it is by guided tour and only open on Thursday to Monday. The address is Water Lane, Woolsthorpe by Casterworth NG33 5PD, telephone 01476 860338.

Woolsthorpe Manor is a typical early seventeenth-century yeoman's farmhouse, famous as the birthplace of Isaac Newton, who was born here on Christmas Day in 1642. It gives an insight into his world and it quite personal and special. Stand in his bedroom and see the window where he used a prism to split sunlight into the colours of the rainbow, then look out onto the garden to see the apple tree which inspired his theory of gravity. Between the summer of 1665 and the spring of 1667, Newton made two extended visits in order to escape the plague affecting Cambridge. It was his 'Year of Wonders', yet outside the bubonic 'Great Plague' of 1665–6 was the worst outbreak of plague in England since the Black Death of 1348. London lost 15% of its population. In later life, Newton stressed that these enforced absences were the most intellectually fruitful times of his whole life.

I popped into Grantham on the way to the house to see what had inspired Margaret Thatcher. She was born above the shop that sits at the intersection of Broad Street and North Parade (now a chiropractic clinic). It was interesting.

The illustration is by Nick Plackett from Chichester

Bosham in West Sussex

Recommended read: *Rook* by Jane Rusbridge, a highly
descriptive novel set in Bosham

---

osham is a very special place on the shores of Chichester Harbour. It
is known as the place where King Canute is said to have held back
the waves, and also for visitors having their cars submerged in water at
high tide – so be careful where you park. There is a good time to go
(when Chichester Cathedral's flower festival is on in June) and a bad
time (Junior Week at the Bosham Sailing Club in August). Either way, try
and time it for the arrival of Dave in his ice cream van (early afternoon
throughout the summer) as it is the best you will ever taste. He always
parks in the same place, which is on the narrow strip to the water's edge.
I recommend an oyster but beware, the portions are huge!

Accommodation:

The nicest place to stay is the Millstream Hotel, which is a stone's
throw from the waterfront. It is a family owned and run hotel with
thirty-five rooms, and a lovely restaurant specialising in fish. The
grounds and building are very attractive, having grown from three
seventeenth century workers' cottages. The address is Bosham Lane,
Bosham, PO18 8HL. Telephone 01243 573234
(millstreamhotel.com).

Bosham

Pronounced 'Bozzom', it is a picturesque village that has something
for everyone. Thatched cottages sit alongside colourfully painted
houses, with a few grand properties in between. Everything is centred
around the top end of the tidal harbour. At one end is a raised circular
path and at the other a small village green by the sailing club.

A brief history:

Inhabited by the Romans, Bosham was the sixth most important town in Sussex in the eighth century. The legend is that the Danish King Canute sat on a chair surrounded by his courtiers and commanded the waves go back (which they didn't). It is a sad fact that his eight-year-old daughter was drowned in the millstream and is buried in Bosham Church in a Saxon coffin at the foot of the chancel steps. It was from Bosham that Harold set forth in 1064 to negotiate with William of Normandy, a voyage that led to William the Conqueror's return in 1066. Indeed, Bosham Church is depicted in the Bayeux Tapestry, which features this series of events leading up to the Conquest of England by Duke William of Normandy. Not to miss on your visit to Bosham in addition to the church and the quay is Bosham Walk (a small art and craft centre) and a stroll along the footpath alongside the water – going as far as you can manage as there is much to see, both man-made (fabulous houses) and natural (plant and bird life) – followed by a coffee in the café that overlooks the harbour. If you wanted a longer walk, visit fancyfreewalks.org under Bosham Harbour and the Chichester Channel. There is a detailed map, with a clear itinerary. This last involves a short ferry crossing to West Itchenor. The ferry runs on demand daily from 9am to 6pm (usually) from May to September and is very homely ... a dog is often at the helm. You might like to do a portion of the walk just to experience the ride and a drink on the other side.

Other places to visit on the trip:

Emsworth

Like Bosham, Emsworth is lovely. It is now mainly a yachting town but has Saxon origins, and in the Middle Ages it was a busy port importing wine, then later coal, and exporting grain. The main history of the town is linked with both oyster fishing and boat building, and the town still has traditional shipwrights. It is made up of narrow streets, Georgian houses and pretty walled gardens, but what sets it apart is the bracing walk along the promenade with water either side. To access it, walk down past the library and the car park (with loos!) and follow the locals as they follow the snakelike trail, which has information boards along the way. If you have more time, there are lots of trails in Emsworth, including a memorial trail, a town tree trail, and the most well known, an oyster heritage trail. A trail booklet can be purchased from various outlets in Emsworth including Borland Estate Agent, Bookends as well as from the library. The oyster trail is available to download via emsworthonline.co.uk under 'Things to do in Emsworth', item 3. If you want the whole Emsworth experience, there is a 'Coffin Walk', which is 5 miles long and starts at the Square in Emsworth. Visit emsworthwalks.org.

Fishbourne Palace

If you've never heard of this amazing place, it is probably because it is run as a charity, receiving no core government funding. Here you can explore the remains of the largest Roman domestic building in northern Europe with in-situ mosaics and Britain's earliest formal garden. There is a short introductory film that explains the background, a model of what it looked like in its heyday and a room set. What is amazing is that it was only discovered in 1960, when the water board were digging a trench for a new pipe and all of a sudden a beautiful mosaic floor emerged. It is thought that it was built between AD 75 and AD 80. A huge building with four wings each about 100m long. Tiberius Claudius Togidubnus and his people – called Regni – lived there. He was king of this part of Britain in the first century AD. I suggest you buy the guide book as a) it explains everything very simply yet was written by the eminent David Rudkin (obituary *The Guardian* 30th August 2021), and b) for the lovely illustrations. The palace is open May to October on Tuesday to Saturday mainly (I went on a Sunday in late February and it was open, so check before you go) and there is no need to book. The address is Roman Way, Fishbourne, PO19 3QR. Telephone 01243 785859 (sussexpast.co.uk).

Of note, if your visit is close to lunch time go to the Crown and Anchor at Dell Quay (it is just down the road at PO20 7EE) for a delicious lunch with a spectacular view over water. Telephone 01243 781712 (crownandanchorchichester.com).

Chichester is the only city in West Sussex and its only county town. At its centre is the Chichester Cross. This is an elaborate perpendicular market cross standing at the intersection of the four principle streets. It is grade 1 listed building built by Edward Story, Bishop of Chichester from 1477 to 1503. It was built so that the poor people of the region could have somewhere to sell their wares – and as a meeting point.

Having got your bearings, I suggest you start at the cathedral. If you have timed it right, your visit will be when the flower festival is on. The aroma on entry will take your breath away, as will the displays by local schoolchildren hidden behind the more professional looking elevated displays. If you haven't timed it for the festival, there is still lots to see, including the Arundel Tomb (the subject of a Philip Larkin poem), a stained-glass window by Marc Chagall, lovely twelfth century carved panels and the John Piper tapestry (behind the altar).

Next visit Pallant House Gallery, which is just off South Street. Telephone 01243 774557 (pallant.org.uk). It is housed in a beautiful Queen Anne house which still has all the characteristic features such as curved sweeping stairway and beautiful wide doors. There is also a modern extension, which has a collection of twentieth-century British art, with works by artists including Walter Sickert, Lucian Freud, Graham Sutherland and Ben Nicholson. Regular exhibitions are also held through the year.

The town shops are worth exploring as hidden down little side lanes are some fabulous clothes shops. My favourite was Indigo in Baffins Lane which was a small family-run business that had been trading for 24 years, but recently closed unfortunately, but there are plenty of others.

On your way home if you have time:

The Weald and Downland Open Air Museum

This museum needs quite a bit of time to fully explore, although it isn't far away in Singleton (go to West Dean Gardens instead if time is short). The museum has 'rescued' buildings dating from 1300 to 1910 that have been restored and re-sited from other areas in South-East England and it is all housed in 50 acres of the South Downs. It was launched in 1967 by a small group of enthusiasts led by the founder Dr JR Armstrong and was opened to the public in 1970. Since its inception, the museum has won lots of awards, partly because it is as much about learning as just seeing the buildings. Indeed they run various courses from basic building conservation to MSc degrees. Telephone 01243 811363 (wealddown.co.uk).

CRUMLIN ROAD GAOL

MATER INFIRMORUM

ULSTER UNI

THE MAC

HARBOUR STUDIOS

TITANIC MUSEUM

TO THE IRISH SEA

S.S. NOMADIC

H&W

H&W

HARBOUR COMMISSIONERS

ST ANNE'S CATHEDRAL

SSE ARENA

HARLAND & WOLFF SHIPYARD

DIVIS TOWER

CITY HALL

C.S. LEWIS SQUARE

RIVER LAGAN

THE WATERFRONT HALL

ST GEORGES MARKET

CITY HOSPITAL

THE OBSERVERS

QUEEN'S UNIVERSITY

ORMEAU PARK

BELFAST
(CENTRE OF)

The illustration is by Peter Martin of Peter Paints Pictures from Northern Ireland

Belfast in Northern Ireland

Suggested read: *Being Various: New Irish Short Stories*
edited by Lucy Caldwell, a tapestry of Irish stories –
some rather unsettling

This trip is memorable in lots of ways – and has the benefit of no car being needed as everything is within walking distance. The best flight to take is British Airways to George Best Belfast City Airport followed by a short bus ride (Europa route 600) to the city terminal, which is directly behind the recommended place to stay. When you book your flights also buy entry to the Titanic Experience for the following day (early if possible – it is fabulous).The website is titanicbelfast.com and the phone number 028 9076 6386. I also suggest you book a table at the Crown Liquor Saloon for your last night on 028 9024 3187 nicholsonpubs.co.uk.

Accommodation:

The Jurys Inn is ideal for this trip. It is located on Great Victoria Street just down from the Opera House. The phone number is 028 9053 3500 and the website jurysinn.com. Although a chain, and big (270 bedrooms), it has a relaxed atmosphere and a very friendly staff. From here, stroll down to the tourist information centre (known as Belfast Welcome Centre) in Donegall Square just two minutes away – taking in the sights along the way including the stunning city hall. In the pack of leaflets you collect, try to include one called 'Historic Belfast', a city centre architectural walking trail. I don't suggest you do it as there are forty-eight buildings featured, but it has the best summary and a comprehensive map.

Suggested itinerary:

The flight I took meant there was only one full day in Belfast over and above the afternoon of arrival and the morning before leaving. It worked out well because half a day is ideal for a rapid immersion in getting a 'feel' for a place. To this end I took the uncomfortable – but necessary – trip down Falls Road to Shankhill seeing the Peace Line, which is the 6 metre high barrier that has divided West Belfast's Catholic and Protestant communities for more than four decades. Black cabs can be booked for 'the Troubles' tour, but on foot with a good map (starting at Castle Street, which becomes the Falls Road continuing to Springfield) you will see the memorial gardens, Sinn Fein headquarters, and various murals on the side of buildings. Look out for Conway Street to gain access to the Peace Line. That evening I had a contemplative meal at Fish City, an award-winning fish and chip shop off Victoria Square (fish-city.com) Telephone 028 90 231 000. The meal was served on their own printed newspaper, which was full of interesting facts including: 'The first fish and chips in Ireland were sold by an Italian immigrant, Giuseppe Cervi, who mistakenly stepped off a North American-bound ship to Queenstown (now Cobh) in Country Cork in the 1880s and walked to Dublin, where he started selling fish and chips outside Dublin pubs.'

The Titanic Experience

One full day with three Belfast destinations: Hopefully – with a ticket in hand – you will follow my lead and be first in the queue for the amazing experience of the Titanic. Everything about it is great ... the building is beautiful, it is in a quiet part of town (with water everywhere), it has a pleasant café and the exhibition itself is phenomenal. I loved it. Opened in 2012 at a cost of £101 million, it won the prize for the World's Leading Tourist Attraction in 2016 (see their Instagram account @titanicbelfast). It charts the story of the Titanic from conception, to construction, to launch and then to the tragedy of her maiden voyage. The two best aspects as far as I was concerned were the ride (sounds tacky ... but it isn't at all), and the recreated cabins, which were researched to the minutest detail for each of the three 'classes' of passenger. It is an education in social history as much as anything else. Even the shop was great. I bought a card for my mother, which had the front page of an American newspaper from the time. The summary on the back was as follows 'The luxury liner RMS TITANIC sank on April 14–15, 1912, en route to New York City from Southampton, England during her maiden voyage. The vessel hit an iceberg about 400 miles (640km) south of Newfoundland causing a 300 foot gash on her starboard side. Over 1,500 lives were lost and only 705 persons survived. The great ship, at the time the largest and most luxurious afloat, was designed and built by Belfast firm Harland & Wolff'. The souvenir guide is worth buying as it goes into specific detail and has poignant photographs.

The Linen Hall Library Café

The second destination was a chance find and a delightful follow-on from the Titanic. Requiring lunch, I couldn't face anything too filling (having had a muffin in the café earlier) or too 'ordinary', and saw a little board near to the welcome centre back in Donegall Square with 'Linen Hall Library Café' on it. It is a best kept secret – despite five-star reviews. Up steep steps into the historic library, it is like stepping back in time. An old parlour, with smiling parlour maids carrying heavy jugs of tap water. Sit in the window if you can, and anything you order will be lovely. I had grilled halloumi with a salad. The website is linenhallcafe.com – they don't take bookings as it is walk in only.

It would be sacrilegious to leave without visiting the library itself as it is the oldest in Belfast (founded in 1788), located in a Victorian former linen warehouse, and the last subscribing library in Northern Ireland. It is known for its Irish and Local Studies Collection, including 350,000 items relating to politics with an archive of the recent Troubles. I was drawn to others areas in the library, including a section on 'Extraordinary Women' (having nearly bought a bookmark in a shop around the corner with famous Irish writers photographs on it, all twelve were men). It goes beyond celebrating female writers and is a collection-based heritage project supporting communities 1965 to today, which is funded by the National Lottery (among others). It was after this I bought the recommended read for Belfast in Waterstones … be warned, it isn't very cheerful, but having visited Belfast it explains a lot and some of the stories will shake you up a little. The other book I nearly suggested is called *Look! It's a Woman Writer! Irish Literary Feminism 1970–2020* by Elis Ni Dhuibhne, but you can sit and read sections of it whilst still in the library.

The Ulster Museum

The third destination is the Ulster Museum, located in the Botanic Gardens at BT9 5AB. Telephone 028 9044 0000. It is huge – 8,000 square metres of public display space with a rich collection of art, history and natural sciences, all with free entry. There is so much to see it is almost overwhelming, so plan first, and be prepared to stand most of the time as for some strange reason there were no seats, even in front of video films lasting several minutes. I sat on the floor and got some strange looks! Having whizzed around, walk back through the gardens, where there is plenty of seating and beautiful things to look at, such as the glass Palm House. This was designed by Charles Lanyon and is one of the oldest examples of a curvilinear cast-iron glasshouse, having been built c1830. The park leads toward Queen's University, which is lovely in itself – as are the houses nearby. Walking on you will discover a vibrant section of the city in the Queen's Quarter. This southernmost part of the city is full of cafés and restaurants with an upbeat vibe. Take a map, as it is easy to get distracted and lose your way.

The Crown Liquor Saloon

After a freshen-up, try to have a drink (and a meal if you've booked) at the Crown Liquor Saloon just over the road from the hotel and the Opera House. It is a stunning building, dating back to the 1880s with mahogany booths, etched glass and gas lighting. It is a former gin palace. When it fell into disrepair, John Betjeman was influential in encouraging the National Trust to take it on, describing it as a 'many coloured cavern'.

Crumlin Road Gaol

A 'must visit' before you leave: Crumlin Road Gaol 53–55 Crumlin Road, BT14 6ST (crumlinroadgaol.com). The phone number is 028 9074 1500. Crumlin Road Gaol closed in 1996, ending a 150 year history of imprisonment, conflict and executions in the Victorian grade A listed building. An estimated 25,000 people were imprisoned here, including murderers, suffragettes, loyalist and republican prisoners. It witnessed births, deaths, marriages, floggings, escapes, hunger-strikes, riots and was used as a depot for the transportation of convicts to Australia. Following extensive renovation it is now open to visitors. There is a very good self-guided tour (best to use the headphones). What I found most poignant was the graveyard. Seventeen men were buried (two were later exhumed) in unmarked graves in unconsecrated ground on the perimeter of the gaol. On the boundary wall alongside, some of the men's initials can be seen etched into the stone – the only visible record of their final resting place and put there by their fellow prisoners.

Cambridge

The illustration is by Laura Jones

Cambridge in Cambridgeshire

Recommended read: *Bluestockings* by Jane Robinson, more of a social history than a story, but nevertheless very good

---

This city is perfect for a two day trip, and ideally go when the students are still there. Early October works well – when the weather can be lovely and the trees are turning colour. It is necessary to book ahead for the Fitzwilliam Museum, King's Chapel and Kettle's Yard (details below), and possibly Anglesey Abbey – to be sure. I also recommend taking a good map as the tourist information office has closed.

Accommodation:

My suggestion is to stay in a great 'aparthotel' that has recently been built near Girton College off Huntington Road. Called Turing Locke, it is described as 'A sleek, avant-garde aparthotel in the brand new, sustainable district of Eddington; 180 spacious apartments – perfect for families, friends, solo travellers and colleagues.' I booked a one bedroom suite, which was fabulous, but a studio apartment would suffice. All of the apartments come with cooking facilities and if you wish to eat out, next door is Kota kitchen and bar (in the Hyatt Centric), where there is also access to a pretty roof terrace. The Locke brand is one to watch as they are growing fast, yet totally committed to sustainability – without abandoning aesthetics. Once there I abandoned my car as buses run every ten minutes into Cambridge from outside the door. The address is 47 Eddington Avenue, Eddington, Cambridge, CB3 1SE. Telephone 01223 618813, and the website is lockeliving.com. To book in before 4pm involves paying a surcharge, so I visited the National Trust property Anglesey Abbey prior to arrival.

Anglesey Abbey and Gardens

Anglesey Abbey is a National Trust property in the village of Lode, about 5 miles to the north of Cambridge. It includes a country house, which was built on the remains of a priory, 98 acres of gardens and a working mill. The priory was closed in 1536 during the Dissolution of the Monasteries and a Jacobean-style house was built on the site of the ruins in about 1600. Owners down the centuries included Thomas Hobson, three local clergymen, and the last private owner was Lord Henry Fairhaven, who lived there from 1926 to 1966. He made extensive additions to accommodate his collection of furniture, art, books and decorative objects, as well as landscaping the grounds. When he died he left the house and its contents to the National Trust.

I started my visit with lunch in the café – which was furnished with clear resin chairs with grasses encased within. It was then that I realised there was more to the place than first meets the eye and rushed off to buy the guidebook (which is a piece of art in itself). It seems that to understand Lord Fairhaven's life it is essential to start with his maternal grandfather, Henry Huttleston Rogers, a successful American businessman from Fairhaven, Massachusetts. He accumulated $100 million by the time of his death in 1909. He was one of the richest people in the world. He had two daughters and the eldest Cara married Urban Broughton, a respected English businessman and engineer, and they moved to England in 1929 with two sons, Huttleston and Henry. Once adults, the brothers bought Anglesey Abbey partly because of its location close to Newmarket racecourse (and their stud near Bury St Edmunds), and also because it happened to be the best land for shooting. Huttleston and Henry agreed that whoever married first would sell their share to the other brother. Hence when Henry married in 1932 he became the sole owner. The guidebook makes fascinating reading, as he liked everything to be accurately timed, neat, tidy, clean and 'just so'. He wore a fresh carnation every morning that he personally selected from a special tray specifically for that purpose. Royalty were regular visitors.

I would have liked to know more about his wife, but surprisingly she was never mentioned, however, it is noted that he was very kind and generous to his employees, so don't leave the kitchen without reading the hand typed note from the gardener. It is quite special.

The house is closed in winter, so do check before you go through the website angleseyabbey@nationaltrust.org.uk. The address is Qay Road, Lode, Cambridge, CB25 9EJ. Telephone 01223 810080.

Not to miss when you visit Cambridge:

The Fitzwilliam Museum

I planned the first day with three things in mind. Firstly breakfast at Fitzbillies, where they sell delicious Chelsea buns (located near to where the bus stops at the kings Parade end of Trumpington Street – just ask the driver), secondly a stroll around Cambridge followed by a visit to the Fitzwilliam (get there for 10am at the latest) and finally by a timed ticket into King's College and Chapel. Day two involved a visit to Cambridge University's botanic gardens and Kettle's Yard.

The Fitzwilliam Museum was founded in 1816 with a bequest from Viscount Fitzwilliam to the University of Cambridge, where he had studied. The museum houses over half a million artworks and artefacts, all displayed in a beautiful listed building. Its treasures range from fine art (including works by Titian, Rembrandt, Canaletto, Monet, Degas and Picasso), to antiquities from Ancient Egypt, Greece, Rome and Cyprus, to furniture, ceramics, silver, armour, music and manuscripts – the list is enormous. The reason it is necessary to book is regular exhibitions are held in a gallery and they are highly prized. There are long queues if you don't get there early. I visited when 'Gold of the Great Steppe' was on. It was amazing. Entry is free and the shop is great for unusual presents. The address is Trumpington Street, CB2 1RB, (fitzmuseum.cam.ac.uk) telephone 01223 332900. Check before you go for the opening times, and surprisingly entry isn't from the main entrance so walk on beyond to the find small glass entry atrium.

King's College and Chapel

A good time to visit is early afternoon, and if you didn't book ahead there is a visitors' centre dedicated to King's just over the road where you can buy a ticket (and also a map, which has a summary of all the colleges on the back as well as a list of all the Nobel Prize winners and lots more interesting information).

King's College was founded in 1441 by Henry VI, who had founded Eton College the year before and subsequently linked the school to King's in order to supply college scholars. It is rumoured that he refused to set foot in the city to lay the foundation stone, because he was so unpopular in Cambridge at the time that he feared he might be assassinated. His unpopularity is not surprising, as he had ordered the demolition of approximately a quarter of the medieval city in order to make way for the college. The land went all the way down to the river, so it restricted access to an important trade route. It also included the city's thriving market place. The chapel was started in 1446 but due to the unstable political climate it was almost a hundred years before in was finished. Work stopped and started in the reign of Henry VII, and Henry VIII finally finished it. The chapel is the last and finest Gothic building to be erected in Europe. According to the information on the back of the map, it is 88 m long, 24.4 m high and 12.2 m wide (with the most amazing fan-vaulted ceiling). Above the alter is Ruben's 'The Adoration of the Magi' (1634), which was given to the college in the 1960s. When inside, do visit the Chapel of All Souls, which was converted in the 1920s into a memorial chapel for the members of the college who fell in the wars of 1914 and 1939. Rupert Brooke's name is there.

On leaving the chapel, use the map and information on the back of the flier to explore the grounds and wander down to see punting on the river. If you go with a friend and the weather is good – maybe hire one. Then before you head back to your accommodation, do look at the Corpus Clock on King's Parade. The website for King's is kings.cam.ac.uk/visit/your-visit, telephone 01223 331100, and for punting scudamores.com. Telephone 01223 359750.

The Botanic Gardens

This heritage-listed botanic garden was originally conceived by Charles Darwin's mentor and teacher, Professor John Henslow. It was opened in 1845 and the plant collection numbers over 8,000 species from all over the world, displayed within 40 acres of beautifully landscaped gardens. It is a gem. Look at the website botanic.cam.ac.uk, where there is a short film about the garden, and plan accordingly. It is an easy walk from the Fitzwilliam and the address is 1 Brookside, Cambridge, CB2 1JE. Telephone 01223 336265. It is open throughout the year, except for between Christmas and the New Year, but opening times vary so check before you go.

Kettle's Yard

Kettle's Yard is a 'private' house with a permanent collection of twentieth-century art that was created and compiled by Jim Ede, once a curator at the Tate Gallery. On the same site is a gallery showing a changing programme of art exhibitions, a café and a fabulous gift shop.

Kettle's Yard House is more than just an art collection, as the building and the way in which the art and other objects are displayed is unique. He positioned and arranged everything himself, being mindful that the space between objects is as important as the objects themselves. It retains the characteristics of a real home and visitors are welcome to sit in the chairs, read the books and enjoy the art at close proximity. It feels very personal, and the collection of art is phenomenal (as is the architecture of the extension within the property). It is critical to book in advance as each group is tiny so there are rarely tickets at the door. My guide was amazing. The house is open Tuesday to Sunday 12–5pm. Telephone 01223 748100 (kettlesyard.co.uk).

Our Community Map of Glasgow!

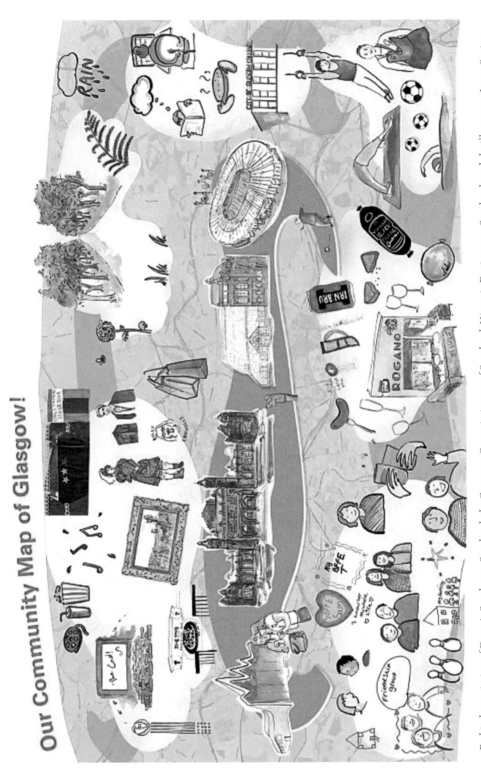

By kind permission of Down's Syndrome Scotland, the Congress Commissioners of Scotland, Historic Enviroment Scotland, and the illustrator Jenny Speirs

'A little bit of a self-portrait, a bit of personal history – made with drawings, photographs, words, shapes and glitter.'

Glasgow in Scotland

Suggested read: either a gentle read, *Eleanor Oliphant is Completely Fine* by Gail Honeyman, which is set in Glasgow, or the tougher *Our Glasgow: Memories of Life in Disappearing Britain* by Piers Dudgeon

Last but not least, with a specific focus on Charles Rennie Mackintosh – involving a fabulous train ride along the Clyde to Helensburgh – is Glasgow. I took the Caledonian overnight train from Euston, and had a lovely cabin and a half-decent sleep (apart from a fire alarm at 4am – hopefully not to be repeated. You could add *Anglo-Scottish Sleepers* by David Meara to your reading list).

Nothing on this trip needs booking in advance apart from the accommodation and the two suggested places to eat, both of which are close by, the first being the Ox and Finch in Sauchiehall Street (oxandfinch.com) and the second Six by Nico in Argyle Street (best to ring on 0141 3345661). It might also be wise to check that a booking isn't needed for coffee at the Willow Tea room (0141 2041903). When planning your trip, do take your National Trust card, warm shower-proof clothing, and definitely purchase a street map (ideally Collins Discovery Glasgow, which can be found by the till in WHSmith at Glasgow station). One of the highlights of my visit was having breakfast in a very stylish hotel – stumbled upon by chance at 7.50am – in West Regent Street on Blythswood Hill, called Dakota (dakotahotels.co.uk). It isn't far from the station and easy to find with the map. Look out for the life-sized string dog in the foyer, and enjoy the best porridge ever!

Accommodation:

I stayed in an upmarket guest house 'The Alamo' overlooking Kelvingrove Park to the west of the city. The location couldn't be faulted and it was peaceful in the extreme, with some luxurious rooms (book room 5 if you can). It has an interesting history, as the whole tenement building was built in 1880 by a wealthy timber merchant. It changed hands over the years until the Gryzbowskis bought it in 1967 to let out rooms. The name was chosen because one of their ancestors had fought at the Alamo Battle in San Antonio, Texas, 1836. I notice the guest house has just been put on the market to sell, so if it reverts to a residential house in the future, try to stay nearby. The address is 46 Gray Street, Kelvingrove Park, Glasgow (alamoguesthouse.com) and the post code is G3 7SE. Telephone 0141 3392395. The key to this trip is dedicating the whole of the middle day to visiting Helensburgh (with a stop at the transport museum and the harbour on your return). Otherwise it was a case of seeing the Mackintosh side of central Glasgow, the Kelvingrove Art Gallery and Museum, and visiting other sites like the university and the gardens close to the guest house.

A brief summary of Charles Rennie Mackintosh in Glasgow:

The presence of Mackintosh is everywhere in Glasgow – hence the focus. Before setting off it is worth looking at the Charles Rennie Mackintosh Society website (crmsociety.com), as it has photographs and a summary of all the venues in Glasgow. Born in Townhead, Glasgow in 1868, he was the fourth of eleven children and his father was in the police force. From an early age he was determined to be an architect, and ill-health as a child enabled him to pursue his artistic interests and ambitions whilst recuperating. After finishing school, Mackintosh was apprenticed to a local architect, John Hutchinson, then in 1889 joined the bigger practice of Honeyman & Keppie. Throughout his apprenticeship and employment, he also took evening classes at the Glasgow School of Art.

It was during his time at the Glasgow School of Art that he started to become more aware of architecture outside of Scotland. With the school's library filled with the latest journals and magazines, Mackintosh's exposure to his international contemporaries saw his talents rise, and in 1890 he won the Alexander Thomson Travelling Studentship with his design for a public hall – allowing him to take an architectural tour of Italy.

Back home in Glasgow, Mackintosh was beginning to make a name for himself with early commissions, including the Glasgow Herald Building (1894) and Martyr's Public School (1895). In 1896 he gained his most substantial commission, to design a new building for the Glasgow School of Art. This was to be his masterpiece and was constructed in two phases in 1897 and 1907. The building was an eclectic mix of styles, most noteworthy the library, which owed much to traditional Japanese interiors. The building is being restored following the terrible fire in 2018.

In Europe the originality of Mackintosh's style was quickly appreciated, and in Austria and Germany in particular he received much acclaim for his work. His architectural designs were judged to be of such a high standard that they were later reproduced as a portfolio of prints. The remainder of his career is described below (as quoted from the CRM Society website).

Throughout his career Mackintosh relied on just a handful of patrons and supporters. The Glasgow businesswoman Catherine Cranston proved to be one of his most influential and her series of tearoom interiors (designed and furnished between 1896–1917) provided him with a virtual freedom to experiment. Responsible for their 'total design' Mackintosh provided the tearooms with furniture (including the dramatic high-back chairs), light fittings, wall decorations and even the cutlery.

Despite success in Europe and the support of clients such as Blackie and Cranston, Mackintosh's work met with considerable indifference at home and his career soon declined. Few private clients were sufficiently sympathetic to want his 'total design' of house and interior. He entered the competition to design a cathedral for the City of Liverpool (1902) but although his design showed a Gothic quality as requested, his entry was rejected and his design for Scotland Street School (1906) in Glasgow was to be his last public commission.

By 1914 Mackintosh had despaired of ever receiving the level of recognition in Glasgow that he felt he deserved. He became increasingly obstinate and incapable of compromise and it is known that this exerted unnecessary pressures on his colleagues. In an attempt to resurrect his career, Mackintosh resigned from the practice and with his wife Margaret Macdonald moved to London.

This was unfortunate timing, for with the onset of the First World War all building work was severely restricted. Adventurous plans for a suite of artists' studios and a theatre were never built. However, after making adjustments to the exterior of a mid-terraced house at 78 Derngate in Northampton (1916), the client W J Bassett-Lowke commissioned Mackintosh to redecorate a number of the building's interiors including the Guests' Bedroom (1919). These designs show him working in a bold new style of decoration and construction, using primary colours and geometric motifs. It was an output of extraordinary vitality and originality but it went virtually unheeded.

A move to the South of France in 1923 signalled the end of Mackintosh's three-dimensional career and the last years of his life were spent painting. He died in London on 10 December 1928.

It wasn't until after his death that his true originality and skill was fully recognised, and why a visit to the Hill House in Helensburgh should be high on everyone's list.

Not to miss when you visit:

The Hill House in Helensburgh

By far the best way to visit is to get the train from Charing Cross Glasgow (an easy walk from the guest house) to Helensburgh Central. It is unbelievably inexpensive for a lovely 45 minute ride along the Clyde. On arrival pop into the tourist information centre in the town

(2 minutes away in Sinclair Street) and pick up a leaflet called 'Helensburgh's Hinterland' then take a short taxi ride to the house. The house is widely recognised as the most iconic of the properties designed by Mackintosh. It was commissioned in 1902 by the publisher Walter Blackie for his family home. Every detail internally and externally was carefully thought out – from the study by the front door (so as not to disturb), to the servants' quarters to the side (not seen or heard), to little nooks and crannies (to escape and read).There are guides in most of the rooms but it is worth buying the guidebook – and visiting the café – whilst there.

It is a category A listed building and belongs to the National Trust of Scotland. On my visit is was encased in scaffolding due to major water ingress – but there was a viewing platform to see the exterior at close quarters and admire the gardens and the view. The house is open throughout the year from 10am–5pm with a few exceptions, so do check before you go through the website nts.org.uk. The address is Upper Colquhoun Street, Helensburgh, G84 9AJ. Telephone 01436 673900.

The suggestion is you then walk back into the town (all downhill) with the tourist information leaflet in hand as it identifies other architecturally significant houses en route, culminating in an amazing Arts and Crafts building which was Clyde Street School and is now part of the New Civic Centre. Indeed Helensburgh itself is full of surprises, so worth spending time there before heading back to the station.

The Riverside Transport Museum

On the train ride back from Helensburgh alight a station earlier at Partick and follow the signs to the Riverside Museum. It is housed in a spectacular waterfront building designed by the architect Zaha Hadid, which was nominated for a major Art Fund Prize in 2012. Purpose built to contain Glasgow's internationally significant transport collection, it also highlights the town's industrial heritage. The Tall Ship Glenlee, built on the River Clyde in 1896, is berthed alongside and can be seen in full view from the restaurant at the rear.

The area of particular interest to me was a recreated street c1895–1930 and the shop displays from 1930 to 1980. The museum has similar opening hours to Hill House but check before you go via glasgowmuseums.com. The address is 100 Pointhouse Place, Glasgow, G3 8RS. Telephone 0141 2872720. On leaving the museum follow the path towards the exhibition centre (SEC) where the COP26 was held. You will see the Armadillo building and the SSE Hydro, which lights up in the evening. It is an interesting and historic part of town with the giant Finniestone Crane, and the Clyde Arc otherwise known as the Squinty Bridge.

Kelvingrove Art Gallery and Museum

The whole area around Kelvingrove is worthy of discovery. Not only is the park lovely, so is the main university building, which is in the Gothic revival style by George Gilbert Scott. I spent time in the Kelvingrove Art Gallery and Museum. It comes under the bracket of 'undiscovered', yet it is close to most Glaswegians' hearts and free to enter. The mythology is that it was accidentally built back to front and that, when it was complete, the architect was so disappointed he jumped to his death from one of the building's towers. The truth is that it was always intended to face into the park whose name it shares. So do view from both sides. The scale inside is daunting, as there are about twenty-two galleries. The Mackintosh room pales in comparison with Hill House, but the Expression galleries were amazing. Collections of French nineteenth century paintings include Monet, Gauguin and Renoir. The museum is open throughout the year from 10am–5pm with a few exceptions. Visit glasgowlife.org.uk. The address is Argyle Street, Glasgow, G3 8AG. Telephone 0141 276 9599.

The Willow Tea Rooms

The famous and original tea room can be found in the heart of the city at 217 Sauchiehall Street. Designed in 1903 for Miss Cranston, it is the epitome of the style that Mackintosh is most well known for. The high-back chairs (that annoyingly some people hang their coats on), the colours, the stained glass and the general feeling of airy spaciousness. You should be able to walk in for coffee around 11am but to be sure telephone 0141 2041903 or email bookings@mackintoshatthewillow.com. The gift shop on the ground floor is rather special too – look out for a pretty little book called *How to tie a scarf.*

If there is time:

The Botanic Garden

At 730 Great Western Road, G12 OUE, and open from dawn to dusk is a lovely garden. Founded in 1817 by Thomas Hopkirk it has several glasshouses, including one designed by John Kibble, which houses the national collection of tree ferns. There are self-led trails around the gardens which cover 20 hectares, with a collection of over 9,000 different plants. Enjoy.